WORLD WAR II
Nazi's Strike

WORLD WAR II
NAZI'S STRIKE

Published by Bookmart Ltd 2005

Blaby Road,
Wigson,
Leicester,
LE18 4SE
Books@bookmart.co.uk

All notations of errors or omissions (author inquiries, permissions) concerning the content of this book should be addressed to TAJ Books 27, Ferndown Gardens, Cobham, Surrey, UK, KT11 2BH, info@tajbooks.com.

ISBN 1-84509-167-1

Printed in China.
1 2 3 4 5 08 07 06 05

CONTENTS

INTRODUCTION   6

THE PATH TO WAR   12

TEST OF WEAPONS: THE CONDOR LEGION   32

WHO'S WHO OF NAZI GERMANY   34

CHRONOLOGY OF WORLD WAR II   109

Hitler and his cabinet.

The first of the Panzers: the PzKpfw I was only armed with two MG13 machine guns.

The cost of World War II is incalculable in human or financial terms. Estimates indicate that about 55 million people died in Europe during World War II; of these, about 8 million were German.

Death was not just for soldiers—civilians died in their millions too, and came from many different directions through these cruel years. In the opening stages of the war, as the German armies invaded Poland, Hitler wasted little time in organizing the killing of large numbers of non-combatants. He wanted to minimize the potential for trouble making amongst the Polish people, and so he tasked Himmler with eliminating the political and cultural elite. Since the job was effectively wholesale murder, it was given to the SS rather than the regular army. Several units of 400 to 600 men were assembled—these were not fighting forces, but death squads. Called Einsatzgruppen, their role was to go in after the invading armies had passed and arrest and murder certain categories of civilians. These included government officials, aristocrats, priests, and business people. The squads also sought out Jews and forced them into overcrowded ghettos. The final death toll of Polish Jews was over three million, but another three million or more non-Jewish Polish civilians also died in the war. This amounted to losing around 18 percent of its prewar population—this was a greater toll than for any other country in the world.

Originally there were plans to ship the German Jews to Madagascar where they would be corralled in special colonies. This became impracticable once war had started, especially when millions more Jews were captured in the occupied countries of the east. Instead, Hitler and Himmler decided that mass

German troops stream into Poland spearheaded by armoured forces. The first Blitzkrieg (lighting war) attack of World War II started at 0445 hours on September 1, 1939. By October 3 Polish resistance had been overcome.

extermination was the answer, and so the Holocaust began. The Nazi's "Final Solution" killed in the order of 6 million Jews, as well as countless homosexuals, the mentally ill, German political prisoners and Bolsheviks. On top of this, a million Serbs were executed and around 1.5 million Romanies died during the period 1933–45. It is estimated that the Nazis executed about 12 million civilians in all.

There were death camps at Auschwitz-Birkenau, Belsen, Treblinka, Sobibor, Majdanek, Dachau, Chelmno and many others elsewhere in Germany and Poland. These camps were run by Himmler's Special Duty Section (Sonderdienst or SD) who

supervised mass exterminations in the killing chambers which they disguised as showers. These had been specially developed to kill large numbers of civilians with a gas called Zyklon-B, a form of cyanide. The dead were then searched for gold teeth; their bodies were often also boiled up to extract fat, which was used to make soap or candles.

At the end of the war these camps were so filled with the dead and the dying that they were serious health hazards to the local population, even after the survivors had been rescued. Belsen, for instance, had to be burned to the ground by British forces with Crocodile flamethrowing tanks to prevent the spread of diseases such as typhus.

As the war progressed, the need for slave labor meant that

many of those who were sent to the concentration camps were forced to work in terrible conditions in German armaments factories. Vast numbers died as the result of starvation, disease and maltreatment. As the war drew to a close, the Nazi hierarchy tried to hide evidence of the concentration camps and slave labor units from the advancing Allied armies.

Even as the Red Army reached Berlin, the death toll of non-combatants continued. Not only did the Russians treat the German civilians they encountered with extreme brutality, but the millions of artillery shells that they fired into the city killed nearly a quarter of a million people during the last three weeks of the war. The atrocities the Russians committed on German civilians can be partly explained as revenge for the treatment that Germany troops had exacted on the peasant population of the Soviet Union. The Russians had cause to be bitter for many other reason too, however. In all, about 5 million Russian soldiers were captured by the Germans, but the brutality they experienced at the hands of their captors killed around 3 million of them. The death toll also continued after the war was over—Stalin sent many of them to labor camps for the crime of being captured, where another million of them died. It is thought that the Soviets lost about 13 million soldiers and 8 million civilians in all.

All the other countries that were involved in the conflict lost large numbers of people. Some, like the British also had troops from the Empire and Commonwealth where there was not much fighting on home soil, and so for these countries the civilian toll at 60,000 was low in relation to the 452,000 soldiers killed. Other countries like Czechoslovakia, however, did relatively little

fighting, losing "only" 10,000 soldiers, but they lost an incredible 330,000 civilians. Yugoslavia lost 300,000 fighting men, which was bad enough, but its civilian population experienced a terrible 1,300,000 losses. Many of these occurred when Hitler ordered the destruction of Belgrade in revenge for their brief uprising.

The toll continues—even small countries like Romania lost 200,000 soldiers and 465,000 civilians. British civilian losses at 60,000 were almost entirely due to bombing and rocket attacks, but nearly half a million military men died. Mussolini's eagerness to get involved in the war cost Italy 330,000 soldiers and 80,000 civilians. Hungary for her part lost 120,000 soldiers and 280,000 civilians. France, whose population had been severely depleted in World War I lost a further 250,000 soldiers and 360,000 civilians. Officially the French government also executed 4,500 collaborators, however, an estimated 50,000 more were executed by the French Resistance.

The numbers are so large that they risk becoming meaningless—it is estimated that approximately 25 million soldiers died during the years 1939–45. Of these, some 19 million were killed in Europe, and around 6 million in the war against Japan. The Allied military and civilian losses were in the order of 44 million, and the Axis lost about 11 million. The numbers got much worse in the Far East—the Chinese lost over 11 million to fighting, with up to another 20 million killed by Japanese. The Americans got off relatively lightly—since they experienced no domestic fighting, their civilian losses were insignificant, although they did lose over 400,000 soldiers.

World War II was truly global—in all, 61 countries with

1.7 billion people took part; this amounts to three-quarters of the world's population. 110 million people did military service, with the major participants being the USSR at 22–30 million, Germany at 17 million, the United States at 16 million, the British Empire and Commonwealth at 9 million, Japan at 7 million and China at 5 million.

The financial cost of World War II can only be estimated. It is possible to calculate how much money was spent by the various governments who took part during and after the conflict—some assessments make this figure more than a trillion dollars. This does not, however, take into account the enormous amount of damage done to privately owned property.

The U.S. spent more than any other country, at an estimated $341 billion. This figure includes $50 billion for lend-lease supplies, which is made up of $31 billion to Britain, $11 billion to the Soviet Union, $5 billion to China, and a further $3 billion to 35 other countries. Germany spent $272 billion, the Soviet Union $192 billion, Britain $120 billion; Italy $94 billion and Japan $56 billion. Official Soviet figures show that the USSR lost 30 percent of its national wealth. In total, the war cost Japan an estimated $562 billion.

What cannot have a financial value placed on it, however, is the change in the balance of world power. Before the war, there were four great military nations—these were Britain, France, Germany, and Japan.

Although America and the Soviet Union were massive countries, they had small armies. Both had experienced terrible poverty and domestic social problems in the run up to the war

German cycle patrol takes cover during the Norwegian campaign.

as a result of major economic troubles. During the war, however, they built up their military machines to such an extent that when the conflict ceased they stood head and shoulders above everyone else, and the term "superpower" was coined.

During the war America and the Soviet Union had a common enemy in the Nazis, and they fought together to entirely eliminate the Third Reich. However, this mutual understanding soon evaporated in the post-war era, and matters went downhill rapidly. This resulted in what became known as the "Cold War," which had a major influence on world politics for several decades thereafter.

In order to punish those responsible for the behavior of the Third Reich during World War II, a war crimes tribunal was held at Nuremberg between November 1945 and August 1946. Although many senior Nazis had escaped 21 did not, and they appeared before Allied judges to answer charges made to them. Only 3 were acquitted, the other 19 being found guilty. Of these 12 were executed, and 7 were imprisoned.

New Year reception for the Diplomatic Corps, 1934.

Since it was always Adolf Hitler's intention to go to war, he knew that a major rearmament process had to be undertaken before his forces could take on the might of the Allies. Germany was, however, bound by the terms of the Versailles Treaty, and this expressly forbid any such rearmament. Ever since the end of World War I, Hitler had been making use of the resentment felt by the vast majority of the German people towards the settlement terms of the peace treaty. In order to rally popular support and to test the resolve of the Allies, he once again played the unfairness card by announcing that Germany would withdraw from the League of Nations. His excuse was that the other European nations did not permit Germany equality in armaments. His propaganda machine had generated enough support for him to be able to afford to go to the people in a plebiscite, and his estimation of the mood was justified when 95.1 percent of the electorate backed his decision.

In 1935, Hitler further risked foreign aggression when he announced that Germany was going to rearm with the creation of a peacetime army of 36 divisions. This clearly violated the terms of the Treaty of Versailles, and the allies met to form a new pact against the fresh threat from Germany. The meeting was held in the town of Stresa, in Italy, and the agreement became known as the Stresa Front. To back this up, several other pacts were initiated. France did a deal with the Soviet Union, which then in turn signed a pact with Czechoslovakia. Hitler knew, however, that he would be able to turn the various countries against each other when the time came. He started by doing a deal with Britain over limits to the size of the German navy. The deal that was

Official photograph for the state visit by Julius Gömbös, Prime Minister of Hungary.

finally struck was in clear breech of the Treaty of Versailles, which angered both France and Italy—Hitler, however, was delighted.

Hitler's plan to weaken the Stresa Front had worked, and he hoped that this would mean he would be able to get away with reclaiming the Rhineland. If he did so, it would not only violate the Treaty of Versailles, but also the Locarno Pact, in which the Germans agreed to comply with the demilitarization of the Rhineland. Hitler knew that the Allies wanted to avoid going to war, but he also knew that his forces were not strong enough to fight them. In March 1936, he followed his instincts, and sent his troops in to the Rhineland; in order to stave off any reprisals from the Allies, Hitler offered non-aggression pacts to France and

Hitler after the New Year reception for the Diplomatic Corps, 1934.

Belgium, and even said that Germany would rejoin the League of Nations. To his great relief, the Allies merely made verbal condemnations, and did nothing more.

As part of the rearmament process, Hitler tested his troops and the vast amount of new military equipment that had been secretly developed by supporting the Nationalists in the Spanish Civil War. This began in July 1937, and as far as the Nazis were concerned, also served to test the reactions of the allies. A further benefit was that Germany was joined in the effort by Italy—this further weakened the Stresa Front, but once again, the Allies demonstrated a "do nothing" policy, an attitude that was to have serious repercussions in the very near future. The fact that German troops were exposed to action on the Iberian Peninsula was very significant—it acted as a glorified military exercise, and allowed them to hone large numbers of raw recruits into well-practiced soldiers. The Spanish Civil War ended in 1939, with victory going to the Nationalists, led by Franco—thanks in part to German and Italian support.

During rearmament, Germany did its best to align itself with as many potential allies as possible. In November 1936, it signed the first part of the Anti-Comintern Pact with Japan. The Comintern or Communist International was an international association of national communist parties which was originally founded in 1919. Its stated aim was to foster world revolution, but in reality it was an organization that allowed the Soviet Union to exert control over the international communist movement. In 1937, the pact was extended to include Italy; the right-wing regimes in Germany and Italy had much in common, and in late

Hitler and Reich Foreign Minister von Neurath.

Hitler and Mussolini in Venice, 1934.

1937 the two countries also signed the Rome-Berlin Axis Treaty.

At this time Hitler was not only busy dealing with foreign affairs—he had tired of sharing power with the remaining conservatives, and in February 1938, replaced Foreign Minister von Neurath as well as the other leading conservatives—this left the Nazis in complete political control. The next part of Hitler's personal agenda was to ensure that the military would follow his orders as he stepped up pressure on the allies with his territorial demands. To do this he used dirty stories dragged up by Heydrich as excuses to sack Blomberg and Fritsch who were the two top commanders of the armed forces, and took over personal command of the military.

With the Rhineland reclaimed, and full control of the army under his belt, Hitler decided that the time had come to annex Austria. Although the Nazi Party was banned in Austria, they enjoyed much popular support there. The man who brought in the ban was the previous Chancellor, a man called Engelbert Dollfuss—in retaliation, the Nazis had murdered him in 1934. His replacement Chancellor Kurt von Schuschnigg did not like or trust Hitler either, and in an attempt to smooth the waters, Hitler sent his predecessor Franz von Papen to act as his ambassador. Matters improved when an agreement was reached in which Germany recognized Austria's sovereignty and in return Austria would acknowledge itself as a "German State" and 17,000 Nazis would be released from her prisons.

Hitler then tried intimidating Chancellor Schuschnigg into reinstating all the Nazi politicians that he had removed from the government, and installing Nazi Artur von Seyss-Inquart as

Hitler signs papers in the Chancellery; with him is Viktor Lutze who became chief of staff of the SA after Röhm's assassination.

Hitler and the French ambassador, André François-Poncet.

Hitler at the New Year reception for the Diplomatic Corps, 1934.

Hitler with the Polish Foreign Minister Colonel Beck.

Hitler confers with his press chief, Dr. Otto Dietrich.

Anthony Eden and Sir John Simon (British Foreign Minister) discuss German rearmament with Hitler, von Neurath and von Ribbentrop. The result of the talks was the Anglo-German Naval Treaty of June 1935.

Hitler signs the Munich Agreement.

Neville Chamberlain returns to England waving a piece of paper that he thought meant, 'Peace in our time.' As we know, it didn't.

Minister of the Interior. He was given just three days to accede to Hitler's demands, which eventually he agreed to, more out of appeasement than anything else. He was, however, disturbed to hear that Hitler had given a speech in the Reichstag, saying that he was not going to recognize Austria's sovereignty after all, and that Germany was responsible for all the German citizens currently in Austria. Schuschnigg decided to put the matter before the people, and set March 13 for a referendum—this was simply going to ask "Are you in favor of a free and German, independent and social, Christian and united Austria?"

While this would appear to be a fair way for the people to show their opinions on the matter, Hitler was not interested in such niceties. When he heard about Schuschnigg's plans, he flew into a rage and ordered his troops into Austria—agreement or no agreement. This sudden annexation became known as the Anschluss. When the troops of the German Eighth Army arrived on the morning of March 12, they received a massive welcome, with vast crowds cheering and shouting. Hitler himself arrived shortly afterwards, and when he reached his home ground at Linz, he was cheered by over 100,000 people. When a new referendum was held on April 10 to ask for the people's opinion on Austria's unification with the German Reich, the vote was officially given as being 99.75 percent in favor.

Preparations for war—1: The 1935 Nuremberg Rally saw an expression of Germany's refound military might. These photographs show anti-aircraft teams ranging in on Luftwaffe aircraft overhead. The Luftwaffe would play a major part in Wehrmacht early war successes.

Preparations for war—2: German naval power was scuttled at Scapa Flow at the end of World War I. In the 1930s she tried to revive her navy (the lower photograph shows the launch of the Admiral Graf Spee*) and coastal defences. But it would be Kriegsmarine U-boats that proved the most effective German naval force.*

Hitler visiting the fleet.

Once again the allies stood by and did nothing—their own domestic problems were taking priority over foreign affairs, which only served to whet Hitler's appetite for more. In September 1938, Neville Chamberlain—the British prime minister, went to Adolf Hitler's home in Berchtesgaden to discuss German demands for the Sudetenland. Hitler stated that unless the allies acceded to his demands, Germany would invade Czechoslovakia. This resulted in crisis meetings with the French and Czechs, after which Hitler was told that his proposals were unacceptable. He met with Chamberlain again, and told him that all Czech troops, police officers, and administrative officials had to leave the area straight away. On top of this was a long list of other demands, including that Czechoslovakia must hand over more territories to Poland and Hungary; the deadline was October 1.

Hitler knew that Britain and France were unlikely to go to war on their own over territorial demands for parts of Czechoslovakia, however, he was conscious that if they allied with the Soviet Union, it would be very bad news for Germany. On Mussolini's suggestion, a conference was held in Munich where representatives from Germany, Britain, France and Italy discussed the current situation. By holding the meeting on German soil, Hitler was able to ensure that neither Czechoslovakia nor the Soviet Union would be present—this minimized the risk of a pact between the allies and the Soviets. He also managed to allay fears of further territorial expansion by promising that this would be the last demand he would make. Both Britain's Neville Chamberlain and France's Edouard Daladier were desperate to avoid war, and used Hitler's promises of future non-aggression as an excuse to hand

Wehrmacht Day at the Nuremberg Rally of 1935.

over the Sudetenland. The transferral, which became known as the Munich Agreement, infuriated the Czechs, but they were bluntly told that Britain would not go to war over the Sudetenland.

This act of appeasement pleased those who believed Hitler's promises that he wouldn't make any further territorial claims, since it seemed a new European war had been avoided. Hitler, however, had other ideas. When the German troops arrived in the Sudetenland, they were greeted by cheering crowds, but not everyone was happy to see them on Czech soil. Emil Hacha was installed as the new president after the previous one resigned, but in March 1939, not long after he took power, Hitler told him at a meeting that German troops would march into Czechoslovakia

In March 1935 Hitler repudiated the terms of the Treaty of Versailles, announcing that he would build an army of half a million men. This is the parade that celebrated Germany's rearmament.

The business end of the Admiral Scheer. *She carried two three-gun turrets armed with 11-inch guns and had a secondary armament of eight 5.9-inch, six 4.1-inch AA and eight 3-pdr AA guns.*

Naval march-past on Wehrmacht Day at the 1935 Nuremberg Rally.

German Junkers Ju52 aircraft over Nuremberg. The Ju52 would be the Luftwaffe's transport workhorse during World War II.

Göring revelled in his position as Luftwaffe supremo.

at 6am the following morning. He was given a stark choice—either tell the Czech army not to resist, or the country would be destroyed. Under much duress, Hacha gave in and the next day silent crowds watched the German invaders march in.

With the German invasion of Czechoslovakia in March 1939, however, it became obvious to even the most naïve that the Nazis were now intent on further territorial conquests. The new target was Poland, and once again Hitler sought a pretext for an invasion. In this case he used a strip of land called the Polish Corridor as his excuse—this was a region which separated Germany from East Prussia which had been given to Poland after World War I. Hitler demanded that the port of Danzig—which was within the corridor, return to German ownership. This time, however, the Allies realized that appeasement was no longer an option, and Poland flatly refused to give Danzig up. As Hitler prepared his forces for an invasion, Neville Chamberlain declared that Britain and France would go to the aid of Poland if Germany should attack. When Hitler heard this he declared, "I'll cook a stew that they'll choke on!"

Hitler knew that he could not simultaneously fight a war with the Soviets as well as the Allies, even though he had every intention of invading Russia. He blamed the Soviets for colluding with the Jews to bring down Germany, and so wanted to end the Bolshevik regime. To buy some time, he arranged a non-aggression pact between Germany and Russia—this basically stated that after Poland had been invaded, Stalin and Hitler would divide the country up between them. Russia would also gain the Baltic states of Latvia and Estonia. The deal which was known as

March 7, 1936, and German troops march into the demilitarised Rhineland over the bridge at Mainz.

either the Nazi-Soviet Pact or the Molotov-Ribbentrop Pact was signed on August 23, 1939.

Hitler once again used his security services to create a suitable excuse to send troops into Poland. The ingenious Heydrich had some of his SS officers disguise themselves as Polish soldiers—they then attacked a German radio station in Gleiwicz. These soldiers then announced on live radio that Poland was invading Germany, and Hitler suddenly had his pretext for invasion. German troops invaded Poland on September 1, 1939, and after Hitler rejected demands to withdraw, Britain and France declared war on Germany on September 3, 1939—World War II had begun.

Spanish refugees in France.

When the Spanish Civil War broke out in 1936, General Franco asked Germany for help. In particular, he needed to get his troops from North Africa and on to the Spanish mainland. Since the Spanish fleet was in the control of the communists, he needed some other way to get them across the Straits of Gibraltar. In response, Göring and Hitler discussed the matter urgently. They both agreed that the spread of communism had to be stopped, and Göring wanted the chance to test and refine his fledgling Luftwaffe. In the end they decided to send a volunteer unit of Germany's air force to support the Nationalists under Franco as part of the fight against Bolshevism. This force was called the Condor Legion, and it was sent to Spain at the end

of July 1936. Hitler also sent 30 Junkers Ju52 transport planes from Berlin and Stuttgart to Morocco. These transported over 15,000 troops to Spain over the space of a couple of weeks, and in doing so made a massive difference to the fortunes of Franco's army.

In the early stages the Legion was effectively a token presence of 26 aircraft, but the numbers increased rapidly over the coming weeks. By November the Legion was comprised of 100 aircraft and 5,000 men under the command of Hugo Sperrle. When the Legion first arrived it was mostly equipped with the Heinkel He51 fighter—this was a biplane and therefore of a very old design. As German aircraft factories started delivering the latest designs, however, they were sent to Spain for combat testing in the Condor Legion. In this way the Heinkel He111 bomber and Messerschmitt Bf109 fighter saw their first active service. This not only allowed the pilots to learn how to fly the new planes, but also to develop the best tactics for using them. As more and more of these fast monoplanes arrived, the old biplanes were switched to ground attack roles, and then finally for use as trainers. The Condor Legion was not just an air force, however, as it included both tank units, gunners and naval personnel. While the sailors trained the Nationalist naval forces, the gunners used their newly designed 88mm heavy anti-aircraft artillery for everything from shooting down enemy aircraft to destroying communist tanks and fortifications. The gun proved to be so effective that it became a major tool of the German Army in WWII.

At first the world took little notice of Germany's contribution to the war; however, when the Condor Legion bombed the seemingly peaceful town of Guernica, on April 26, 1937, the sheer scale of the destruction brought fierce international condemnation. Over 1,000 civilians were killed and 60 percent of the town destroyed. Later that year in the Asturias campaign, Adolf Galland further contributed to the misery of the Spanish people when he started experimenting with a new tactic which became known as carpet bombing. The results of these raids were analysed and refined for maximum effect—the outcome was that when WWII started, the blitzkrieg offensives were launched with devastating efficiency.

While the German contribution to Franco in the Spanish Civil War was far smaller than that provided by Italy, it still had a massive effect. Not only did the Nationalists get military support

General Francisco Franco.

when they needed it most, but Hitler was able to prolong the war to his own ends. He succeeded in drawing Italy closer to Germany as well as getting many of his troops trained in the realities of war and his military equipment tested and refined. He also managed to get a friendly power installed in a strategically important location, along with its important supplies of mineral ores and other useful resources. Although Germany's involvement was financially expensive, as far as Hitler was concerned it was money well spent.

Adolf Hitler

It has been claimed that Adolf Hitler's deranged character was the product of his upbringing—he had an overly strict father to whom physical beatings were simply how you disciplined an unruly child. Hitler's mother tried to compensate for this by being overly affectionate, and when she died, he was absolutely devastated. He became fixated with anti-Semitism before the start of World War I, and when Germany lost, he—like many others, blamed the Jews. By using this as his rallying cry, he built up a large following, and he soon proved to be a hypnotic public speaker. He also gained popular approval by claiming that the Versailles Treaty should be rescinded, that war profits should be confiscated and that the Jews should lose their civil rights. On top of this he wanted recent Jewish immigrants to be expelled, and stirred up further hatred by claiming that the dire state of the economy was their fault

Throughout the early 1920s Hitler exploited public resentment at Germany's treatment at the hands of the Allies, and built up the Nazi Party with illegal mass protest rallies until it became a strong political force. Hitler then over-stepped the mark by attempting to stage a coup—this was known as the Beer Hall Putsch, and its failure resulted in him spending a year in prison. While he was locked away, he wrote Mein Kampf, where he presented his ideas on the future of the German peoples—and in particular how the Communists were in league with the Jews in an international conspiracy.

He reserved his real fury for his claims that the Jews were an anti-race hell-bent on the perversion of true German

Hitler was a remarkable orator who mesmerised his audience both with his rhetoric and his charismatic presence.

Hitler was much-photographed, particularly by Heinrich Hoffmann, whose photographic assistant, Eva Braun, would eventually become Hitler's wife.

blood—specifically he said that they wanted "the promiscuous bastardization of other peoples." The only way to stop them was to eliminate them, and by taking over their lands, the Germans would gain badly needed Lebensraum—living space. This was a particularly popular message with the vast numbers of people who were suffering in the overwhelming financial crisis the country was experiencing.

Hitler continued to gather support until he was made chancellor in 1933. From this point on he continued to strengthen his position by the use of murder, intimidation, deceit and intrigue. By the late 1930's he had built up the German economy by putting the entire country on a war footing. He ordered his armed forces to annex Austria and the Sudetenland in 1938, and then invaded Poland on September 1, 1939.

Such military action forced France and England to declare war on Germany, but this did not deter Hitler from going on to take most of Western Europe by using Blitzkrieg (lightning war) tactics. He then went on to invade the Soviet Union in August 1939, but early successes were reversed when the Russian winter took its toll on German forces, in particular with defeats at Moscow in December 1941 and Stalingrad through the winter of 1942-43. This coincided with America entering the war following the Japanese attack on Pearl Harbour, and was followed by total defeat in North Africa. This led to the Allies invasion of Italy and ultimately the re-taking of France in 1944. During this period the combined allied air forces destroyed most of Germany's industrial capacity and many of her towns and cities .

Despite many attempts on his life, Adolf Hitler survived until

Hitler on his 47th birthday, April 20, 1936.

the Red Army entered Berlin. On April 30, 1945, when it was clear that all was lost, he married his mistress in a last-minute ceremony and then shot himself. He left behind him a Europe devastated by years of war, terror campaigns and racial cleansing.

Adolf Hitler with Eva Braun.

Eva Braun

(1912-1945) Hitler's mistress from 1932 and his wife during the last few hours of his life, Eva Braun was born in Munich, the daughter of a school teacher. Of middle-class Catholic background, she first met Hitler in the studio of his photographer friend, Heinrich Hoffmann (q.v.), in 1929, describing him to her sister, Ilse, as "a gentleman of a certain age with a funny moustache and carrying a big felt hat."

At that time Eva Braun still worked for Hoffmann as an office assistant, later becoming a photo laboratory worker, helping to process pictures of Hitler. The blonde, fresh-faced, slim, photographer's assistant was an athletic girl, fond of skiing, mountain climbing and gymnastics as well as dancing.

After the death of Geli Raubal, Hitler's niece, she became his mistress, living in his Munich flat, in spite of the opposition of her father who disliked the association on political and personal grounds. In 1935, after an abortive suicide attempt, Hitler bought her a villa in a Munich suburb, near to his own home, providing her with a Mercedes and a chauffeur for personal use. In his first will of 2 May 1938 he put her at the top of his personal bequests—in the event of his death she was to receive the equivalent of £600 a year for the rest of her life.

In 1936 she moved to Hitler's Berghof at Berchtesgaden where she acted as his hostess. Reserved, indifferent to politics and keeping her distance from most of the Führer's intimates, Eva Braun led a completely isolated life in the Führer's Alpine retreat and later in Berlin. They rarely appeared in public together and few Germans even knew of her existence. Even the Führer's closest associates were not certain of the exact nature of their relationship, since Hitler preferred to avoid suggestions of intimacy and was never wholly relaxed in her company.

Eva Braun spent most of her time exercising, brooding, reading cheap novelettes, watching romantic films or concerning herself with her own appearance. Her loyalty to Hitler never flagged. After he survived the July 1944 plot she wrote Hitler an emotional letter, ending: "From our first meeting I swore to follow you anywhere--even unto death--I live only for your love."

In April 1945 she joined Hitler in the Führerbunker, as the Russians closed in on Berlin. She declined to leave in spite of his orders, claiming to others that she was the only person still loyal to him to the bitter end. "Better that ten thousand others die than he be lost to Germany," she would constantly repeat to friends.

On 29 April 1945 Hitler and Eva Braun were finally married. The next day she committed suicide by swallowing poison, two minutes before Hitler took his own life. On Hitler's orders, both bodies were cremated with petrol in the Reich Chancellery garden above the bunker. Her charred corpse was later discovered by the Russians.

THE TOP NAZIS
Martin Bormann

Martin Bormann was a ruthless manipulator who used every dirty trick in the book to reach the highest levels of the Nazi Party—and through their use even became Hitler's most trusted aide. He made many enemies as he deviously rose through the ranks of the Nazi hierarchy and became what Hitler called his most "loyal party comrade."

Born on June 17, 1900, in Halberstadt, Germany, Martin Bormann was only 14 when World War I began—nevertheless, before it ended he joined up as a artilleryman. After hostilities ceased, he became a member of the Rossback Freikorps, a small extremist right-wing political party. Bormann showed his true colors whilst he was still only in his early twenties, when he took part in the murder of one of his former teachers as the man responsible for the capture and execution of a senior Freikorps member. For this, Bormann served one year in prison, after which he joined the Nazi Party as a press officer. He soon showed promise, and before long had risen to become a business manager.

After marrying the daughter of a senior Nazi Party member, Martin Bormann's career took off, and he became one of the elected Nazi delegates in the Reichstag when Hitler came to power in 1933. He then took a post as Rudolf Hess's personal secretary with the title of Chief of Cabinet in the Office of the Deputy Führer. In this position, he had access to the highest levels of government, and quickly came to Hitler's attention when he realized that extra party funds could be generated by charging royalty fees for the use of Hitler's image on postage stamps.

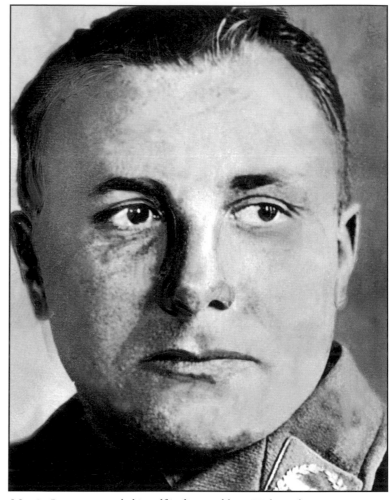

Martin Bormann made himself indispensable to Hitler as his private secretary. His death was not witnessed although in April 1973 a German court formally pronounced him dead after exhuming a skeleton half a mile from Hitler's bunker.

On top of this he managed to create a special fund into which industrialists who were profiting from Nazi rearmament could contribute cash to the Nazi party. Between them, these two ideas raked in million, and unsurprisingly, Hitler was very impressed.

Bormann enjoyed having access to power, and decided that the best way would be to get closer to Hitler. He did this by

Hitler's HQ staff during the attack on the West: to Hitler's left is Jodl and then Bormann.

slowly taking over Hess' duties—he always carried a notebook, and whenever Hitler gave a verbal order or made a suggestion, Bormann wrote his thoughts down and saw to it that they were carried out. In this manner he made himself indispensable, and he became one of Hitler's most trusted aides. Hitler was so angered by Hess's abortive attempt to broker peace with the British that he abolished the post of Deputy Führer which Hess had previously held. In its place he created the role of Head of the Party Chancellery, and gave the position to Bormann.

In 1943, he was made Secretary to the Führer, and it was in this role that he started to wield real power. Anyone who wanted to see Hitler had to have Bormann's agreement, and to enhance his situation, he created an alliance with Himmler, who had access to the Gestapo's secret files. Having such information to hand, he was a very dangerous man and was not afraid to get involved in power plays with the likes of Göring, Goebbels, and Speer.

Bormann was indiscriminate in his approach to dealing with the Jews, and ensured that they received the worst of treatment in the concentration camps. He also felt that the Catholic church stood in the way of the Nazis, and did his best to suppress the influence of religion in the Third Reich. To do this he saw to it that he was given jurisdiction over all manner of domestic affairs, including the courts and churches.

When the end came in the spring of 1945, Bormann remained with Hitler—even signing his last will and testament and acting as witness to Hitler's marriage to Eva Braun. After Hitler committed suicide, Bormann left the bunker—some say he escaped to South America, others that he was killed by a Russian anti-tank shell while he was trying to escape. This would appear to be backed up by the facts—one of two skeletons dug up in Berlin in 1972 was positively identified as that of Martin Bormann.

Dr. Hans Frank, Nazi Governor-General of the General Government of Poland.

Hans Frank

Born in Karlsruhe on May 23, 1900, Frank was a Nazi lawyer—Hitler's lawyer—who became the governor of the Generalgouvernement of Poland from 1939 to the end of the war.

He served for only the last year of World War I and joined the Freikorps afterwards, Frank joined the Deutsche Arbeiterpartei in 1919, and became a member of the NSDAP when it was absorbed. He took part in the Munich Beer-Hall Putsch as a stormtrooper. He passed the bar exams in 1926 and from then on defended brownshirts in court—a full-time job as there were over 40,000 such trials between 1925 and 1933. Throughout the 1920s, Frank served as Adolf Hitler's personal lawyer and the head of the legal department of the NSDAP.

Frank lost his importance as a lawyer after the Nazis reached power in 1933. He was given a number of positions including Bavarian Minister of Justice and Reichsleiter of the NSDAP.

After the defeat of Poland in September 1939, the Germans and Russians split the country into three: the western went to the greater reich; the eastern went to the Soviet Union, leaving the central area—the Generalgouvernement, a semi-independent administrative unit. Frank was appointed governor-general of the Generalgouvernement. However, Frank did not hold great power there. He was the most important administrator in the region; but while he managed to get Hermann Göring to cooperate with him regarding the region's economy, the SS took charge of the extermination of Jews in the Generalgouvernement. Hitler meant for the Generalgouvernement to be used as a "racial dumping ground," an endless supply of slave labor, and a site for the mass extermination of European Jewry. Frank did not oppose these goals, but he hated others infringing on his domain. Thus, he went back and forth, sometimes opposing and sometimes supporting the inflow of Jews and Poles who had been expelled from German-occupied areas and the mass murder of Jews. He very much wanted to please Hitler, but he also wanted to build up his own power base. This conflict led to his downfall.

In March 1942 Frank was stripped of all power over racial and police issues. He then began to openly criticize SS policies, leading Hitler to remove Frank of his party positions. Hitler, though, would not allow Frank to resign, so Frank stayed in the position of governor-general until he was forced to flee from the advancing Soviet army. After the war, Frank was tried and hanged at Nuremberg. His official diary still serves as an important source for World War II historians.

Wilhelm Frick

Wilhelm Frick was born in Germany in 1877. A police officer in Munich, he joined the National Socialist German Workers Party (NSDAP) and took part in the Beer Hall Putsch. Along with Adolf Hitler was found guilty and was imprisoned for his role in the attempted putsch.

In 1924 Frick was elected to the Reichstag where he associated with the NSDAP radicals led by Gregor Strasser. He became the first Nazi to hold high office when he was appointed as Minister of the Interior in the state of Thuringia.

When Adolf Hitler became Chancellor in 1933 he appointed Frick as his Minister of the Interior and was responsible for operating the Enabling Act. He also drafted the Nuremberg Laws, that began the persecution of the Jews in Germany.

Frick was involved in a struggle with Heinrich Himmler and the Schutzstaffel (SS) and in 1943 lost his job as Minister of the Interior. Adolf Hitler now appointed him the Protector of Bohemia and Moravia, a post he held until the end of the Second World War.

Frick was accused of crimes against humanity at the Nuremberg War Crimes Trial. At his trial Frick argued that he had never intended the Nuremberg Laws to be used for mass murder, although he accepted that this is what happened. Wilhelm Frick was found guilty and executed on October 1, 1946.

Walther Funk

Walther Funk, the son of a businessman, was born in Trakehnen, Germany, on August 18, 1890. After studying economics at university he became a financial journalist.

Funk joined the National Socialist German Workers Party (NSDAP) in 1931. He became an adviser to Adolf Hitler and encouraged him to move away from the radical anti-capitalist views of Gregor Strasser and Ernst Röhm.

After the Night of the Long Knives Funk's influence grew and in 1937 he was appointed by Hitler as Minister of Economics.

Two years later he succeeded Hjalmar Schacht as President of the Reichsbank.

During the Second World War Funk collaborated with Heinrich Himmler in depositing money looted from the Jewish community.

At the end of the war Funk was captured by Allied troops. Found guilty of crimes against humanity at the Nuremberg War Crimes Trial he was sentenced to life imprisonment. In May 1957, Funk was released from prison because of ill-health and died in Düsseldorf on May 1, 1960.

Goebbels in his office as seen in Signal *magazine.*

Josef Goebbels

Josef Goebbels was one of the most famous and talented propagandists of all time. Through clever manipulation and presentation of the truth, he was able to help Hitler bring the Third Reich to reality.

Paul Josef Goebbels was born on October 29, 1897, to a poor, but devoutly Catholic working class family who lived in the Rhineland. At the age of seven he fell seriously ill, and following surgery was left with a crippled foot and a left leg that was three inches shorter than the right. This caused him to walk with a pronounced limp, which gave him an real inferiority complex. Although he was rejected out of hand due to his physical

condition when he tried to enlist in 1914, he overcame this humiliation and went and went on to study at eight different universities. During this time he received his Ph.D. in German literature from the University of Heidelberg, and had ambitions of becoming an author.

Goebbels joined the Rhineland branch of the Nazi party in 1924, where his literary talents were quickly made use of. He was soon appointed as secretary to Gregor Strasser, the Nazi party organizer in North Germany, and editor for two important party publications, the Volkische Freiheit (National Freedom), and the NS Briefe (NS Letters). When Hitler saw Goebbels speak publicly, he was very impressed at his ability to work a crowd, and realized that he would be a great asset to the Nazi Party. At first,

Hitler, Magda and Josef Goebbels.

Goebbels felt that Hitler should not be leading the Nazis, and that they should unite with the Communists. Hitler, however, was not to be put off, and through the use of lies, flattery, charm and deceit soon managed to win Goebbels' loyalty—something he demonstrated until the very end.

In 1926, Hitler named Josef Goebbels party leader of Berlin—a job he performed extremely well. From here he went on to become Nazi Party Propaganda Chief in 1930, where he felt that no method was "too crude, too low, too brutal." His work motto became, "Any lie, frequently repeated, will gradually gain acceptance." He gave the German people the message that Hitler was on a divine mission, and that they were racially superior to the "subhuman" Jews and Slavs. Goebbels made the Nazi Party into a pseudo-religious movement and used as many symbolic and ritualistic devices as possible.

Goebbels went on to be appointed Minister of Popular Enlightenment and Propaganda and also created a new agency called the Reich Chamber of Culture, which controlled all aspects of the press. He ensured that free speech was eliminated, and that the film industry glorified Nazi Stormtroopers and vilified the Jews. Goebbels stayed close to Hitler throughout the war, and when the end was in sight he took his wife and six children (ages 5 to 13) to the bunker beneath the Reich Chancellery. After Hitler killed himself, Goebbels and his wife arranged that they and their children would be killed by SS orderlies.

Göring as commander-in-chief of the SA. He is wearing an Ehrhardt Brigade helmet and the Blue Max he won during World War I.

Hermann Göring

Hermann Göring remains one of the better known characters of the Third Reich; he was born into the German aristocracy in Rosenheim, Bavaria on January 12, 1893. His father was a senior army officer, so it was natural for him to be educated at a military school. At the age of 19 he joined the German Army, and when World War I began he served with the infantry until rheumatoid arthritis of the knees hospitalized him. After this he joined the German Army Air Service, where he gained a reputation as an ace fighter pilot, with recorded 22 kills.

After the war, Göring became a civilian pilot, and went on to join the Nazi Party in 1922. As an open admirer of Hitler's, he soon became a leader of the Sturm Abteilung's brownshirts. His social status proved very useful to Hitler, since he had family contacts amongst Germany's leading industrialists. As a result of this, the Nazis were able to persuade many of these influential movers and shakers that the threat from the Bolsheviks was so great that the only way to prevent a collapse into Communism was to support the Nazis.

Göring played a small part in the infamous Beer Hall Putsch, but as a result of the medical treatment he was given for shrapnel wounds, he became addicted to morphine. While this did not significantly impair him for many years, later he completely lost control of the addiction. Since the putsch had failed, those who took part were wanted criminals, and Göring was no exception. He fled to Sweden, where he stayed for four years—during this time his health declined and his weight increased dramatically; on his return to Germany he weighed 280lb.

Göring's family connections undoubtedly helped him receive an amnesty from President Paul von Hindenburg in 1927, whereupon he returned to Berlin. Within a year he had been elected to the Reichstag as one of 12 Nazi Party members, and in August 1932 he was made President of the Nazi Party. When he became Chancellor, Hitler made Göring a cabinet minister without portfolio, and then not long after, minister of the interior and prime minister of Prussia. This post included control of the Geheime Staats Polizei (GESTAPO), and Göring wasted no time in ensuring the loyalty of these forces by replacing 22 of the 32 chief officers with members of the SA and SS.

Göring was instrumental in terrorizing Hitler's political opponents, and together with Himmler and Heydrich organized the massacre of the SA's leaders in the Night of the Long Knives. After relinquishing control of the Gestapo to Himmler, Göring became head of the German Air Force—the Luftwaffe. At this time it had little military significance, since it was composed of small numbers of trainers and a few prototype aircraft. Göring was responsible for the utter transformation of the Luftwaffe into the most modern and powerful air force in the world.

Incredibly, Göring also oversaw the restructuring of the German economy into a system that was able to afford to rearm all three services (army, navy and air force), as well as create enough prosperity to maintain public morale. Hitler was so impressed by these achievements that he named Göring as his successor in 1939, and in 1940 appointed him to be Reichsmarschall.

All this power and glory turned Göring into an arrogant and

Göring later in the war.

used, and Hitler began to lose faith in him. This situation became much worse when, in contrast to his over-ambitious claims, the Luftwaffe failed to supply the German Sixth Army when they were under winter siege at Stalingrad. Hitler never forgave Göring, and blamed him for all manner of other military problems.

Since he had lost Hitler's respect, Göring spent much of the rest of the war plundering the museums and private homes of occupied Europe for art treasures for his own collections. During this time his morphine addiction got much worse, and began to lose contact with reality. When Berlin was surrounded by the Red Army, Hitler's communication lines were cut off, and Göring tried to implement earlier plans for him to assume command. Hitler considered this to be an overthrow, and had Göring arrested and replaced by Admiral Dönitz.

With the Red Army approaching, Göring surrendered to the U.S. Army in Austria on May 8, 1945. As a leader of the Nazi regime, he was later put on trial at Nuremberg for War Crimes and involvement in Crimes Against Humanity. He was found guilty, but before the sentence could be carried out, he committed suicide by swallowing a cyanide capsule on October 15, 1946.

greedy man. He made vast fortunes from his activities, which included ownership of the Essener National newspaper. When war broke out in the summer of 1940, he further increased his standing by claiming responsibility for the rapid defeats of France, Netherlands, Belgium and Luxembourg. This did not last, however, and he lost credibility by putting too much faith in air power, a problem that was exacerbated by his boastful nature. As a result of this, he made many mistakes in how the Luftwaffe were

Hess and Hitler in Munich before World War II.

Rudolf Hess

Rudolf Hess, became Deputy Führer of the Nazi party, and was Adolf Hitler's most devoted follower.

Rudolf Hess was born in Alexandria, Egypt on April 26, 1894, where his father was a successful exporter and wholesaler. He was privately tutored as a child since his father considered the local Protestant school to lack the necessary discipline. Hess was 20 years old when World War I broke out in 1914, and he immediately volunteered for military service. He started out with the 7th Bavarian Field Artillery Regiment, but then transferred to the infantry where he was awarded the Iron Cross, second class for his courage and integrity. After this he managed to get accepted for the Imperial Air Corps, but shortly after having gone through the aeronautical training, the war ended.

When Hess first saw Hitler at a meeting of the German Worker's Party, he was captivated by Hitler's enormous passion. Hess joined the party straight away and from that moment on was dedicated to advancing Hitler's political causes. The two became close friends during the troubled times of the Beer Hall Putsch and the consequent confinement where they shared a cell at Landesberg prison. It was there that Hitler named Hess as his private secretary. When the Nazis gained power in 1933, Hess was given the titles of Deputy Führer of the Nazi Party, and Reich Minister without Portfolio.

As the war got underway, Rudolf Hess became a victim of

After his flight to Britain, Hess was kept in prison—at first in Britain and postwar in Spandau—until he killed himself in 1987.

Martin Bormann's political intrigues, and soon found that he had lost most of his power and influence. Knowing that Hitler badly wanted to end hostilities with the British, Hess tried to regain Hitler's approval by embarking on a madcap attempt to negotiate a peace settlement with Churchill by personally flying a Messerschmitt Bf110 fighter plane to Scotland in May 1941. He flew to Scotland because at the Berlin Olympics of 1936 he had met Douglas Douglas-Hamilton who became the Duke of Hamilton. Hess had already tried to negotiate a peace with Britain through the duke in 1940, and still hoped that his personal contact would do the trick. The duke had not replied to Hess's earlier advances on the advice of British Intelligence, and when Hess arrived in Britain after bailing out of his aircraft, he was immediately imprisoned, his mission having failed completely.

Churchill—who always viewed Hess as a medical and not a criminal case—ensured he was treated with dignity and he was imprisoned in the Tower of London.

In Germany, Hitler felt betrayed by someone he had previously considered to be a close personal friend—second in line to succeed Hitler after Göring. Branded a madman by his erstwhile colleagues, Hess remained as a prisoner of the Allies for the duration of the war. At the Nuremberg Trials he was sentenced to life imprisonment in Spandau Allied Military Prison, where he hanged himself on August 17, 1987.

Reinhard Heydrich

Reinhard Heydrich turned Germany into a terrifying police state and was responsible for the deaths of millions of innocent people.

Reinhard Tristan Eugen Heydrich was born on March 7, 1904, in Halle an der Saale, Germany. His Catholic family was well off, but strongly anti-Semitic. Although his early years were mostly spent studying music, he also joined the Maracker Freikorps and the Deutscher Schutz und Truzbund, both right-wing extremist groups that were highly racist. He was too young to play a part in World War I, but after the war, at the age of eighteen, he became a naval cadet at Germany's main naval base at Kiel. Within four years he rose to the rank of second lieutenant, and became a signals officer on the battleship Schleswig Holstein. He stayed in the navy until April 1931, when Admiral Erich Räder sentenced him to dismissal for impropriety as a result of seducing the daughter of an influential shipyard director and then spurning her for another woman.

Not long after leaving the navy, Heydrich came to the attention of Himmler, who was looking for someone to set up a counterintelligence branch of the SS. He was given the job, and soon proved to be brilliant in his work, using his cold, calculating mind to invent new methods of trapping, humiliating, and destroying his enemies. His main weapon was a database of dirty secrets that he built up on all manner of people, all stored in a rigorously efficient filing system . These included senior Nazi members as well as their opponents—he obtained information through his own web of informers, which made him especially

The Reichsprotektor of Bohemia and Moravia, Reinhard Heydrich, in Prague in 1941.

dangerous. His work was so important to the Nazis that he was promoted to the rank of SS major within the year, and again to SS colonel a year later. His counterintelligence service was renamed as the Sicherheitsdienst (Security Service, or SD for short).

Heydrich and Himmler worked together for many years, each depending on the other on their quest for power and control. The partnership proved itself to be especially powerful in June 1934 when the two of them decided that the SA was getting too strong. Although Ernst Rohm was one of Hitler's close personal friends, as head of the SA, he posed a significant threat to both Heydrich and Himmler. The SA was, however, also a threat to Hermann

After Heydrich's assassination there were widespread reprisals but none so terrible than the destruction of Lidice where 172 men and boys over 16 were murdered by Nazi troops. This is a postwar remembrance service for the inhabitants of Lidice.

Göring. In return for control over the Gestapo, the SD provided false evidence of an intended SA coup—Heydrich then convinced Hitler to countenance a purge of the SA. It was these actions that resulted in the wholesale slaughter that became known as the Night of the Long Knives.

After the threat from the SA was removed, Heydrich built the Gestapo into a massive organization with even more dirty secrets filed away for future use. Their methods were extreme, and even minor infractions such as anti-Hitler jokes resulted in death sentences. Members of the Gestapo could arrest or murder anyone they wanted, and this instilled a reign of fear that spread throughout Germany. He did favors for Hitler, and as the war progressed continued in his ruthless campaign of terror, all the time acquiring more control over new departments and offices. His reputation was such that he became known as the "blonde beast" and as "Himmler's evil genius."

When the German armies invaded Russia in 1941, Heydrich was responsible for running special killing units—the Einsatzgruppen. These units would go to Jewish villages and murder vast numbers of innocent civilians, usually by single shots to the back of the head. By the end of 1941, it was estimated that between the Ukraine, Latvia, Estonia, and Lithuania, almost half a million people had been massacred. When Heydrich was sent into Czechoslovakia to oversee the situation there, he quickly became known as the "Butcher of Prague" for his barbarous actions. In desperation, the exiled Czech government had two specially trained men parachuted into Czechoslovakia, where with help from the partisans, in December 1941, they managed to assassinate Heydrich with a grenade.

After Heydrich died, Hitler ordered massive reprisals to be made on the local civilian population. He was then succeeded by Ernst Kaltenbrunner, who was a life-long fanatical Nazi. Like Heydrich, he was another brutal man, responsible for the deaths of millions of Jews and political suspects in the concentration camps, as well as the murder of large numbers of prisoners of war. Kaltenbrunner was indicted for war crimes by the International Military Tribunal at Nuremberg and sentenced to death. He was hanged on October 16, 1946.

Heinrich Himmler

After Adolf Hitler, the image of Heinrich Himmler probably represents the persona of the Third Reich more than any other. During his reign of terror he became one of the most powerful people in the world, and was directly responsible for the deaths of many millions of innocent civilians. He was described as "the most unscrupulous figure in the Third Reich," and even Heydrich called him a sadist.

Heinrich Himmler was born in Munich on October 7, 1900, into a strict catholic middle class family. His father was a headmaster who had personally tutored the children of many influential families. As a result of these close ties, Prince Heinrich of Bavaria had agreed to become Himmler's godfather.

Although he was too young to join up for military service during World War I, Himmler played his part by joining an officer cadet unit. His main interests lay in agriculture, and so it was in this direction that he started training after leaving school. He worked on a farm for a while, and then went to Munich University as an agricultural student. After this he started to take an interest in politics— he worked as a technical assistant at a fertilizer company for a while, but then got increasingly involved in the Reichskriegsflagge, a paramilitary group led by Ernst Röhm. He also joined the Nazi Party, and was present at the Beer Hall Putsch, but took no significant part in what happened there.

When Hitler was jailed for leading the failed coup, the party's number two man, Gregor Strasser took control of the northern faction of the party. Himmler was hired by Strasser as his general assistant, which mostly involved keeping the office running and spreading propaganda. Himmler's logistical skills showed through very quickly, and before long he was put in charge of organizing the SS in southern Bavaria. He continued to work his way upwards within the party, and in 1926, when Strasser was made party propaganda chief, Himmler moved with him to Munich as his deputy.

Himmler's fortunes improved further when Hitler appointed him to be National Commander (Reichsführer) of the SS in January 1929, and was especially pleased when the SS was made fully independent of the SA in 1931. Not long after this though, he started to see the SA as rivals to his SS, and together with Göring managed to convince Hitler that Rohm was plotting his overthrow. The result was the Night of the Long Knives, when the SS massacred the SA's higher echelons. After setting up the Race and Resettlement Central Office (RUSHA), he spent a lot of time trying to promote the idea of the Nordic race as superior beings.

In June 1936 Himmler became Chief of the German Police, which further increased his power and influence. He kept building up the SS, by the time war was approaching it had been split into two separate divisions, with one being military (the Waffen-SS) and the other non-military (the Allgemeine-SS). As war broke out, the Waffen SS were used to perform the most brutal atrocities, such as mass executions in civilian settlements, since most of the regular German Army would not stand for such behaviour. The SS were also heavily involved in setting up and running the concentration camps, as well as being responsible for the mass killings of their inmates. On top of this, the SS did much of the organization for the provision of slave laborers for the German

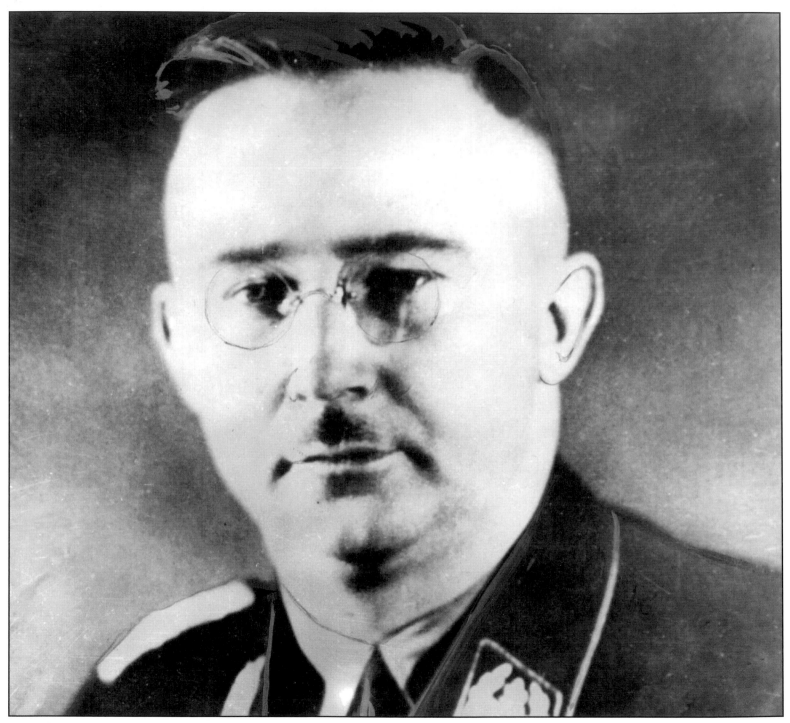

Heinrich Himmler, Reichsführer of the SS and leader of the Gestapo.

war effort.

Himmler was dedicated to purging Germany of all but the purest genetic stock—in an address to his SS leaders, he stated that:

'It is not only the struggle of the nations, which in this case are put forward by the opposing side merely as a front, but it is the ideological struggle of the entire Jewry, freemasonry, Marxism, and churches of the world. These forces—of which I presume the Jews to be the driving spirit, the origin of all the negatives—are clear that if Germany and Italy are not annihilated, they will be annihilated. That is a simple conclusion. In Germany the Jew cannot hold out. This is a question of years. We will drive them out more and more with an unprecedented ruthlessness.'

Through the early stages of the war, Himmler carried on ordering and co-ordinating the deaths of millions of innocent people; Hitler was so pleased with his performance that in 1943 he also made him Minister of the Interior. As the war continued, however, Himmler realized that the Nazis could not win, and he began to negotiate with the Allies behind Hitler's back. He also realized that he could use the large numbers of concentration camp prisoners under his control as pawns in order to broker the best possible deal. This was in spite of the order given by Hitler that none should be allowed to fall into the hands of the Allies.

As the war drew to a close, it became obvious that the Soviets were going to engulf vast areas as they marched on Berlin. The thought of being captured by the Red Army terrified everyone,

junior and senior officers and men alike, and Himmler was no exception. He tried to get the Allies to accept the Nazi's surrender, on the condition that they then joined forces to defeat the Soviets. When Hitler got word that Himmler was talking to the Allies behind his back, he took it as the worst act of treachery that he had ever known. In his will, Hitler wrote:

'Before my death, I expel the former Reichsführer of the SS and Minister of the Interior Heinrich Himmler from the party and from all his state offices. Apart altogether from their disloyalty to me, Göring and Himmler have brought irreparable shame on the whole nation by secretly negotiating with the enemy without my knowledge and against my will, and also by illegally attempting to seize control of the State.'

After the fall of the Third Reich, Himmler attempted to evade the Allies with disguises and false papers. On being sent to a screening camp, he revealed his identity, but on being searched, he bit into a cyanide capsule and died shortly after.

Ernst Kaltenbrunner at the Nuremburg trials.

Ernst Kaltenbrunner

Ernst Kaltenbrunner, the son of a lawyer, was born in Austria on October 4, 1903. He got a doctorate in law from Graz University in 1925 and set up as a lawyer in Linz.

Kaltenbrunner joined the Austrian Nazi Party in 1932 and worked closely with Artur Seyss-Inquart and Adolf Eichmann.

Kaltenbrunner became head of the Austrian SS in 1934 but soon afterwards was arrested and accused of being involved in the assassination of Engelbert Dollfuss. Found guilty of conspiracy and was sentenced to six months in prison.

After Anschluss Kaltenbrunner was elected to the Reichstag and became minister for state security as well as police chief in Vienna. During the next three years Kaltenbrunner served as Commander-in-Chief of the Schutzstaffel (SS) in Vienna.

In April 1941 Kaltenbrunner was appointed Lieutenant-General of Police. He impressed Heinrich Himmler and when Reinhard Heydrich was assassinated in May, 1942, Kaltenbrunner was appointed as head of the SD (Sicherheitsdienst). In this position he not only controlled the Gestapo but also the concentration camp system and was responsible for carrying out the Final Solution.

Nearly seven feet tall, with deep scars on his face from his student duelling days, Kaltenbrunner appeared to obtain pleasure from his work and took personal interest in the different methods of killing the inmates in the extermination camps.

As well as the hunting down and extermination of several million Jews Kaltenbrunner was also responsible for the murder of Allied parachutists and prisoners-of-war.

With the Red Army closing in on Germany, Kaltenbrunner gave orders for all prisoners in extermination camps to be killed and then fled south but was captured by Allied troops. Accused of crimes against humanity at the Nuremberg War Crimes Trial he was found guilty and executed on October 1, 1946.

Robert Ley

Robert Ley (February 15, 1890—October 25, 1945) was a prominent government figure in Nazi Germany.

He was born in Niederbreidenbach, Germany. He studied at the university of Bonn and received a degree in chemistry. During WW I he was a pilot. Shot down in 1917, he spent two years as a French POW. He worked for IG Farbenindustrie after the war, but was dismissed in 1928.

He joined the NSDAP in 1925 and quickly became a Gauleiter. In 1932 he was elected to the Reichstag and also succeeded Gregor Strasser as head of the Reichsorganization der NSDAP. In April 1933 Hitler ordered the suppression of the German trade unions and appointed Ley to head the operations.

In early May troops occupied trade union buildings, union funds were confiscated and union leaders were arrested. The unions were replaced with a single organization, the Deutsche Arbeitsfront (DAF, German Labor Front) which was headed by Ley from May 10, 1933. The Christian trade unions were not reduced in the initial efforts but lasted little more than a month longer.

At the end of WW II Reichsleiter Ley fled to Berchtesgaden but was captured on May 16, 1945 and sent to trial at Nuremberg. But he committed suicide by hanging himself in his cell before the trial proper could begin; "Robert Ley, the field marshal of the battle against labor, answered our indictment with suicide. Apparently he knew no better answer". He had stated, that he could not bear the accusation of being a war criminal.

Robert Ley (1890-1945) German Nazi leader during speech in Berlin Sportpalast.

Adolf Hitler and Heinrich Himmler at the 1934 Nuremberg Nazi Party rally with Victor Lutze, head of the SA (Sturmabteilung). Ca. August - September 1934.

Viktor Lutze

Victor Lutze was born in Bevergen, Germany on December 28, 1890. He joined the German Army in 1912 and fought in the First World War.

After the war Lutz joined the police force. A member of the National Socialist German Workers Party (NSDAP) and the Prussian State Council he was appointed police president of Hanover in 1933.

When Ernst Röhm was murdered during the Night of the Long Knives Lutz became leader of the emasculated Sturm Abteilung (SA).

Lutze remained as police president of Hanover until he was killed in a car crash on the autobahn on May 2, 1943.

Josef Mengele

Dr. Josef Mengele (March 16, 1911–February 7, 1979), also known as the Angel of Death, was a Nazi doctor who performed experiments on prisoners in Auschwitz which were condemned as murderously sadistic and participated in the selections of people to be sent to the gas chambers.

Mengele's nickname was Beppo.

Mengele was the eldest of three sons of Karl Mengele (1881–1959) and his wife Walburga (d.1946), well-to-do Bavarian industrialists.

In 1931, at the age of 20, Mengele joined the Stahlhelm (Steel Helmet); he joined the SA in 1933, and applied for Nazi party membership in 1937. In 1938 he joined the SS, and in 1938–39 served six months with a specially trained mountain light-infantry regiment. In 1940 he was placed in the reserve medical corps, following which he served three years with a Waffen-SS unit. In 1942 he was wounded at the Russian front and was pronounced medically unfit for combat. Because he had acquitted himself brilliantly in the face of the enemy during the Eastern Campaign, he was promoted to the rank of Captain. Afterward he volunteered to serve at a concentration camp, and he was sent to the death camp Auschwitz and became the chief medical officer of the camp on May 24, 1943.

It was during his 21-month stay at Auschwitz that Dr. Mengele achieved infamy, gaining the nickname "Angel of Death." When rail-cars filled with prisoners arrived in Auschwitz II Birkenau, Mengele would frequently be waiting on the platform to personally select which of them would be retained for work and experimentation and which would be sent immediately to the gas chambers.

Josef Mengele left Auschwitz disguised as a member of the regular German infantry. He turned up at the Gross-Rosen work camp and left well before it was liberated. He was then seen at Matthausen and shortly after he was captured as a POW and held near Munich. He was released by the Allies, who had no idea that he was in their midst. Mengele departed for Argentina in 1949, where many other fleeing Nazi officials had also sought refuge, but moved from country to country afterward to avoid

Josef Mengele in Paraguay in 1960. The doctor from the death camp at Auschwitz escaped prosecution and died in 1979.

capture. Mengele divorced his wife Irene, and in 1958 married his brother Karl's widow, Martha, and later she and her son moved to Argentina to join Mengele.

Despite international efforts to track him down, he was never apprehended and lived for 35 years hiding under various aliases. He lived in Paraguay and Brazil until his death in 1979, when he suffered a stroke while swimming in the ocean and drowned. He was not tracked down by Nazi hunters until the mid-1980s, and in 1992 DNA tests on his bones confirmed his identity.

Premier Benito Mussolini of Italy and Chancellor Adolf Hitler of Germany, pictured as they met in Venice, where it is believed the two dictators discussed armaments and other vital questions affecting the political situation of Europe. Baron Von Neurath is seen at the right.

Konstantin von Neurath

Konstantin von Neurath was born in Klen-Glattbach, Germany, on February 2, 1873. After studying law at the University of Berlin he entered the German foreign service in 1903. He was a member of the consular staff in London from 1903 to 1908, before returning to Berlin.

He joined the German Army in the First World War and as a captain won the Iron Cross. After being badly wounded he returned to diplomatic service in Turkey.

After the war Neurath served as Minister to Denmark and Ambassador to Italy. Following a period as Ambassador to Britain (1930-32) Franz von Papen appointed him Foreign Minister. He retained the post under Kurt von Schleicher and Adolf Hitler.

Neurath held right-wing opinions conservative views but had doubts about Hitler's aggressive foreign policy. Hitler kept him in position as he gave the government respectability. In March 1938 Hitler replaced Neurath with Joachim von Ribbentrop when he complained that the current policy would result in war.

In 1939 Adolf Hitler appointed Neurath as Protector of Czechoslovakia. When Czech students protested against Nazi rule Neurath closed all the universities in the country. He also ordered nine of the students who took part in the rebellion to be executed.

Hitler felt that Neurath did not deal harshly enough with the resistance movement in Czechoslovakia and in September, 1941, replaced him with Reinhard Heydrich.

Neurath was captured by Allied troops at the end of the Second World War. At the Nuremberg War Trial he was found guilty of war crimes and sentenced to fifteen years in prison. After serving eight years he was released on account of his poor health. Konstantin von Neurath died on 1 August 4, 1956.

Carl Oberg

Carl Oberg was born in Hamburg, Germany in 1897. He joined the German Army and served in the First World War. After the war he joined the Freikorps and took part in the Kapp Putsch in 1920.

Oberg worked for a tropical-fruit trading company before enduring a long period of unemployment. In 1930 he acquired a tobacco stand in Hamburg.

Oberg joined the Nazi Party (NSDAP) and in 1932 he went to Munich where he worked with Richard Heydrich. He eventually became Heydrich's right-hand man in the SD Security Service.

In 1938 Oberg was given command of an SS (Schutzstaffel) battalion in Mecklenburg. The following year he became chief of police in Zwickau.

On the outbreak of the Second World War Oberg went to Poland and became SS and Police Leader in the Radom district where he was responsible for rounding up Jews and the drafting of Poles for forced labor.

In March 1942, Oberg was promoted to SS-Brigadeführer and two months later was posted to Paris where he became SS and Police Leader in occupied France. In this position he brought in severe measures to deal with the French Resistance including the shooting of hostages. Oberg was also responsible for applying the Final Solution in France. This action resulted in 75,000 Jews being deported from France to extermination camp in Nazi Germany and Poland.

Oberg was promoted to SS-Obergruppenführer and police general in August 1944. Later that year Oberg was posted to the

General Karl Oberg, leader of the SS and Gestapo Chief in Paris, France. He was known as the "Butcher of Paris".

command of a military unit that was part of an army formation commanded by Heinrich Himmler.

In June 1945 Oberg was arrested by Allied troops. The following year he was extradited to France where he was brought to trial. Convicted of war crimes, Oberg was sentenced to death on October 9, 1954. After an appeal, this was reduced to life imprisonment.

President Charles De Gaulle granted Oberg a pardon in 1965. Carl Oberg died later that year in Germany.

Joachim von Ribbentrop

Joachim von Ribbentrop (April 30, 1893—October 16, 1946) was the German Foreign Minister from 1938 until 1945.

Ribbentrop was born in Wesel, Niederrhein, as the son of an officer. Fluent in French and English, Ribbentrop lived several years abroad. He served in the Army during World War I, finally as a first lieutenant, and was awarded the Iron Cross. He then became a diplomat, stationed in Constantinople. A wealthy wine merchant, he joined the National Socialist party in 1932. Two years earlier, in 1930, he had met and impressed Adolf Hitler with his knowledge of foreign affairs. He became Hitler's favorite foreign policy advisor and was a great admirer of Hitler. In 1933 he was given the title of SS-Standartenführer.

He was Minister Plenipotentiary at Large (1935—1936) and negotiated the Anglo-German Naval Agreement in 1935 and the Anti-Comintern Pact in 1936, in August 1936 he was appointed Ambassador to Britain. While in Britain, his son, Rudolf von Ribbentrop, attended the Westminster School in London. In 1938 he succeeded Konstantin von Neurath as Foreign Minister in the German government. He played a role in the German annexation of Bohemia and Moravia (1938), in the conclusion of the Russo-German nonaggression pact, the Molotov-Ribbentrop Pact in 1939, and in the diplomatic action surrounding the attack on Poland.

At the end of World War II, Ribbentrop was dismissed by Admiral Karl Dönitz, but he was a defendant at the Nuremberg Trials and was found guilty by the enemy of all charges they put against him. Since Hermann Göring had committed suicide a

few hours prior to the time of execution, Ribbentrop was the first prisoner of war to be hanged on the night of October 16, 1946. His last words were (spoken in German): "God protect Germany! My last wish is that Germany realize its entity and that an understanding be reached between the East and the West. I wish peace to the world."

In 1953 Ribbentrop's memoirs Zwischen London und Moskau were published.

Alfred Rosenberg

Alfred Rosenberg was a propagandist who was responsible for many of the Nazis policies towards the Jews. He also formed special units which ransacked Jewish properties—especially museums and libraries for art treasures and other valuable artefacts.

Alfred Rosenberg was born in Estonia (which at the time was part of Russia) on January 12, 1893, into the family of a cobbler. As a student he studied architecture in Moscow until the revolution in 1917, whereupon he returned home and got involved in counter revolutionary politics. This resulted in him having to flee to Germany to avoid arrest, where he joined the National Socialist Party in 1919. As a skilled propagandist he started writing all manner of official party material, and in 1921 was also made editor of the official Nazi party newspaper, the Völkischer Beobachter.

Rosenberg argued strongly that preserving German racial purity was of paramount importance, and that the threat from the Bolsheviks justified Germany invading Poland and Russia. He then went on to found the Militant League for German Culture in 1929, and in 1930 was elected to the Reichstag. The same year he published a manuscript called The Myth of the Twentieth Century, in which he claimed that there were two opposing races—the Aryans and the Jews. The Aryans, he said, were responsible for the creation of everything of cultural value, whereas the Jewish race sought to pervert or destroy the very same things. He became head of the Nazi party foreign policy office in 1933, where he called for the Treaty of Versailles to be rescinded.

Portrait of Alfred Rosenberg, the Nazis' ideologist and Reichminister for the Eastern Occupied territories where he arranged the extermination of Jews and slave labour gangs. He was executed following the Nuremberg Trials.

Over the next few years he continued to push his extremist racial beliefs, and his advocacy of German expansion. Hitler was so impressed with his abilities in this area that he appointed Rosenberg to be head of the Hohe Schule, the "University of

Fritz Sauckel

Fritz Sauckel (Ernst Friedrich Christoph Sauckel, October 27, 1894—October 16, 1946) was a senior government official in Nazi Germany. He was General Plenipotentiary for the Employment of Labor from 1942 until the end of the war.

Born in Haßfurt-am-Main, near Bamberg, the only child of a postman and a seamstress. He was educated at local schools and left early when his mother fell ill. He joined the merchant marine of Norway and Sweden, aged just fifteen. He went on to sail throughout the world and rose to the rank of Vollmatrose. At the outbreak of WW I he was on a German vessel en route to Australia when the vessel was captured and he was interned in France from August 1914 until November 1919.

He returned to Germany and found factory work in Schweinfurt. He studied engineering in Ilmenau from 1922 to 1923. He joined the NSDAP in 1923 (member 1,395). He also married in that year and went on to have ten children. He remained a party member over its dissolution and publicly rejoined in 1925. Sauckel was appointed party Gauleiter of Thüringia in 1927 and became a member of the regional government in 1929. Following the Nazi seizure of power in 1933 he was promoted to Reich Regent of Thuringia and Reichstag member. He was also given a honorary rank of Obergruppenführer in the SA and the SS in 1934.

During WW II he was Reich defense commissioner for the Kassel district (Reichsverteidigungskommissar Wehrkreis IX) before being appointed General Plenipotentiary for the Employment of Labor (Generalbevollmächtigter für den

Nazism," in 1940. Under the guise of establishing this spurious academic institution, Rosenberg sent units out to seize books from Jewish libraries as well as art treasures from Jewish homes and public buildings. After the invasion of the Soviet Union had begun in 1941, he became Reich Minister for the Occupied Eastern Territories.

Although Rosenberg operated at the very highest levels of power, and was a supporter of the repression of the Jews, he did try to minimize the harsh treatment of other races in the occupied Eastern Territories. This brought him into direct conflict with the SS, and as a result the overall amount of influence he wielded was reduced. This did not help him when he was captured by the Allies at the end of the war and tried at Nuremberg. He was found guilty on many counts, including war-crimes and crimes against humanity. He was sentenced to death and executed on the morning of October 16, 1946.

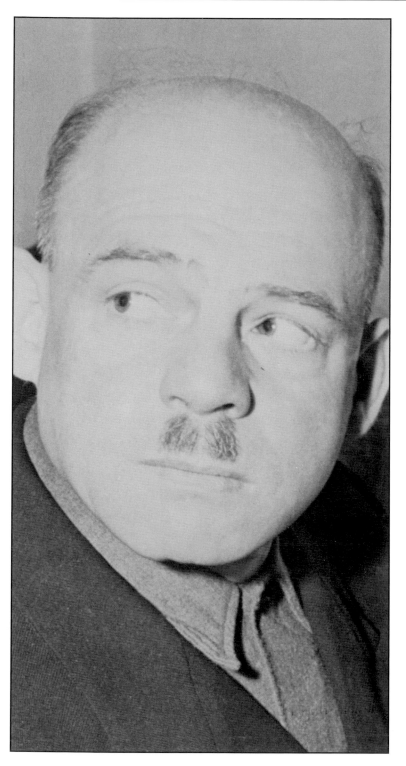

Arbeitseinsatz) on March 21, 1942, on the recommendation of Albert Speer. He worked directly under Hitler through the Four-Year Plan Office. He directed and controlled German labor. In response to increased demands he met the requirement for manpower with people from the occupied territories. Voluntary numbers were insufficient and forced recruitment was introduced within a few months. Of the 5 million workers brought to Germany, around 200,000 came voluntarily. The majority of the acquired workers originated from the Eastern territories, where the methods used to gain workers were reportedly very harsh.

He was a defendant at the Nuremberg Trials accused of conspiracy to commit crimes against peace; planning, initiating and waging wars of aggression; war crimes and crimes against humanity. He defended the Arbeitseinsatz as "nothing to do with exploitation. It is an economic process for supplying labor". He denied that it was slave labor or that it was common to deliberately work people to death (extermination by labor) or to mistreat them.

He was found guilty of war crimes and crimes against humanity, and together with a number of colleagues, he was hanged on October 16, 1946. His last words were recorded as "Ich sterbe unschuldig, mein Urteil ist ungerecht. Gott beschütze Deutschland!" (I die innocent; my sentence is unjust. God protect Germany.)

Artur Seyss-Inquart

Artur Seyss-Inquart (July 22, 1892—October 16, 1946) was a prominent Nazi official in Austria and for wartime Germany in Poland and the Netherlands.

He was born in Stonarov, Moravia, then part of Austria-Hungary. He moved with his parents to Vienna in 1907 and later went to study law at the University of Vienna. At the start of World War I, he enlisted with the Austrian Army in August 1914 and was given a commission with the Tyrolean Kaiserjäger and served in Russia, Romania and also Italy. He was decorated for bravery on a number of occasions and while recovering from wounds in 1917 he completed his final examinations for his degree.

He liaised between the Austrians and Germany for the Anschluss and he joined the German Nazi party in May 1938. He drafted the law reducing Austria to a province of Germany and remained head (Reichsstatthalter) of the newly named Ostmark, with Ernst Kaltenbrunner his chief minister and Burckel as Commissioner for the Reunion of Austria (concerned with the "Jewish Question"). Seyss-Inquart also received an honorary SS rank of "Gruppenführer" and in May 1939 he was made a Minister without portfolio.

Following the invasion of Poland, Seyss-Inquart became administrative chief for Southern Poland, but did not take up that post before the General Government was created, in which he became a deputy to the Governor General Hans Frank. It is claimed that he was involved in the movement of Polish Jews into ghettoes, in the seizure of strategic supplies and in the "extraordinary pacification" of the resistance movement.

Following the capitulation of the Low Countries he was appointed Reichskommissar for the Occupied Netherlands in May 1940, charged with directing the civil administration, with creating close economic collaboration with Germany and with defending the interests of the Reich. He supported the Dutch NSB and allowed them to create a paramilitary Landwacht, which acted as an auxiliary police force. Other political parties were banned in late 1941 and many former government officials were imprisoned at Sint-Michielsgestel. The administration of the country was largely controlled by Seyss-Inquart himself. He oversaw the politicisaton of cultural groups "right down to the chessplayers' club" through the Kulturkammer and set up a number of other politicized associations. Germany demanded occupation costs in the region of 50 million marks per month.

When the Allies advanced into the Netherlands the Nazi regime enacted a scorched earth policy and destroyed docks and harbours to flood much of the country. The civilian population, with much agricultural land useless and with limited transport that could have moved food stocks for civilian use (partly due to civil disobedience), suffered in almost-famine conditions from September 1944 until early 1945, with around 30,000 Dutch people starving to death. Seyss-Inquart remained Reichskommissar until May 8, 1945, when, after a meeting with Karl Dönitz, he was captured in Hamburg.

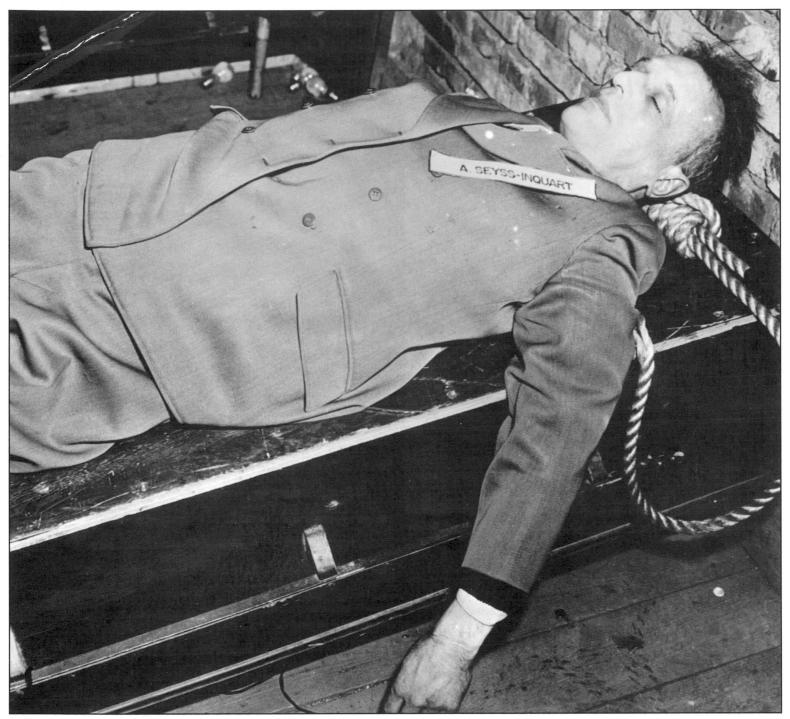

The Nazi war criminal, Arthur Seyss-Inquart, after execution at Nuremberg. He served as Hitler's governor in Austria.

opponent of the rich. The same political beliefs also made him a militant opponent of Christianity throughout his career.

One of von Schirach's great attributes was his ability to inspire enthusiasm in the young, and this combined with his devotion to Hitler, made him a natural choice as the leader of the National Socialist German Students' League, a post he took in 1929. Two years later, he was also appointed as Reich Youth Leader of the NSDAP. Von Schirach was also an excellent organizer, and the endless propaganda helped by the vast youth rallies he staged drew hundreds of thousands of eager new members to the party fold. Out of this massive influx of young blood he built the Hitler Youth or Hitlerjugend into a massive cult—in 1936 it had six million members. The core principles he encouraged were designed to create a new cadre of soldiers ready for Hitler's war machine. These ideals included character, discipline, obedience and leadership, all held together with a powerful mixture of pagan romanticism, militarism and naive patriotism. They were told they were the basis for a new Aryan race of supermen or Übermensch.

Although Baldur von Schirach was incredibly successful in these efforts, it did not make him immune to the conspiracies of other high level Nazis. Jealous of his popularity, he became a target for the likes of Martin Bormann. This undermined his credibility, and he was relieved of his command of the Hitler Youth. He was made Governor of Vienna, Austria in August 1940, and Bormann continued to feed Hitler with misinformation about von Schirach's activities, especially his pleas for better treatment for the people of eastern European. Von Schirach also voiced his disapproval of the manner in which the Jews were being deported,

Nuremberg: inspection of the Hitlerjugend. Behind Hitler is its head, Baldur von Schirach.

Baldur von Shirach

Baldur von Schirach was born in Berlin on March 9, 1907, to an aristocratic German father and an American mother. After a privileged upbringing, he joined the Nazi Party in 1924 whilst at the University of Munich where he was studying Germanic folklore and art history. His strong socialist ideals meant that he did not fit in with his aristocratic peers, and he became a strong

Russian guards on duty outside Spandau prison. Seven Nazi war criminals served sentences in Spandau, each given a number. 1 was Baldur von Schirach; 2 Karl Dönitz; 3 von Neurath; 4 Erich Raeder; 5 Albert Speer; 6 Walther Funk; 7 Rudolf Hess.

but the fact that he was involved in the removal of 185,000 Jews from Vienna to Poland stood against him after the war. At the Nuremberg trials he denied all knowledge of genocide, denounced Hitler as "a million-fold murderer" and called Auschwitz "the most devilish mass murder in history." He was sentenced to 20 years in prison for crimes against humanity, and was released in 1966 after serving them. He wrote in his memoirs that he should have done more to prevent the establishment of the concentration camps. He also accepted responsibility for helping to poison a whole generation of youth, and considered it his duty to stop any ideas of resurrecting Nazism. He died in August 1974.

Hitler visits the site of the House of German Art in Munich. Albert Speer is on the right of the photograph.

Albert Speer

Albert Speer was an architect who rose to become one of Adolf Hitler's closest colleagues. He was tasked with keeping the German war effort running in spite of allied air bombardment and naval blockades. His organizational skills kept the war going for at least a year longer than it otherwise would have, at an untold cost in human lives and misery.

Albert Speer, was born in Mannheim on March 19, 1905. His father was an architect, and after following the usual schooling that the child of a professional family would receive, he went on to study architecture at the Munich Institute of Technology and at the Berlin-Charlottenburg Institute. He became an architect in 1927, and in 1932 became a member of the Nazi Party (NSDAP) after hearing Hitler speak. Shortly afterwards he also became a member of the SS—as a consequence of this he met Adolf Hitler in July 1933, whereupon he was given the task of organizing the 1934 Nuremberg Rally. This included the design of the parade grounds, searchlights, and banners, factors all used to great effect

An older Albert Speer seen with Admiral Karl Dönitz and Generaloberst Gustav Jodl.

in the Triumph of the Will, the famous film created by Leni Riefenstahl. Speer excelled at such matters, and Hitler was so impressed with his skills he was appointed as the Führer's personal architect. Speer was given many important commissions including the German exhibit at the Paris Exhibition in 1937, the Reich Chancellery in Berlin and the Party Palace in Nuremberg.

Speer's efficiency was such that Hitler came to rely on him for many important matters, and in 1942 he took over from the engineer Fritz Todt as minister for armaments. In doing so was given charge of the Organization Todt, which used forced labor for the construction of strategic roads and defences. When Göring fell from favor in 1943, Speer also took over as planner of the German war economy. Under his management, German economic production went up, even in the face of the massive amount of Allied bombing. Speer gained a reputation as a "Good Nazi"—in part, this was due to the fact that he did his best to stop Hitler from destroying German lands and properties in a scorched earth policy ahead of the advancing allied and Soviet armies. Had these plans gone ahead, it would have left Germany ruined.

After the war was over, Speer was sentenced to 20 years in prison at the Nuremberg trials. On his release he wrote his memoirs, wherein he stated that he should have known more about what was going on, but didn't; he died a wealthy man in 1981.

Reich Party Leaders Meet. Nuremberg, Germany: Reichminister Hermann Goering (right) and Julius Streicher, Nazi Jew-baiter No. 1, exchange greetings when meeting at Nuremberg for the 10th Nazi Party Congress.

Julius Streicher

Julius Streicher (February 12, 1885—October 16, 1946) was a prominent Nazi prior to and during World War II. He was the publisher of the Nazi Der Stürmer newspaper, which was to become a part of the Nazi propaganda machine. The newspaper was controversial even in Nazi circles because of its pornographic obsessions and sensationalism. His publishing firm released an anti-Semitic children's book Der Giftpilz (trans. "The Poisonous Mushroom").

During the time of the Munich Beer Hall Putsch of 1923, Streicher became friendly with Adolf Hitler and became an active advocate for him.

He was executed following due process at the Nuremberg war trials in 1946. He shouted "Heil Hitler!" just before the trap door opened beneath him.

THE GENERALS
Johannes Blaskowitz

A professional soldier of the old school who rose to become a Commander in Chief of the German army Johannes Blaskowitz was born on July 10, 1883, in Peterswalde in the County of Wehlau, East Prussia. He saw service in WWI, but it was not until the Third Reich came to power that he rose to prominence. In 1932 he served as the Commanding Officer of the 14th Regiment, and in 1935 he was promoted to become the Lieutenant-General and Commander of Military District II, Stettin. He became the Field Commander of Army Group 3 (Dresden), and was involved in the invasions of Austria and Bohemia, and led the Third Army into the Sudetenland.

Blaskowitz was a key player in the planning of the invasion of Poland, where he later commanded the Eighth Army. After receiving the surrender of Warsaw, on September 27, 1939, he was made Military Governor of the German occupying forces in Poland. Although he was very much a part of the Third Reich, he was outraged by the behaviour of Heydrich's S.D. units and the Einsatzkommandos towards Polish Jews and intellectuals. After producing documents detailing their atrocities, he was relieved of his command by Hitler, who felt that his concern for the welfare of foreign civilians was "childish."

After falling foul of Hitler's displeasure, Blaskowitz kept his concerns to himself and in 1940 served first as the General Officer Commanding the Ninth Army and then as the Military Commander Northern France. He was then transferred to become the General Officer Commanding First Army, France, where he remained until 1944, when he took control of Army Group G, France under von Rundstedt. In this role he prepared to defend the area against the expected Allied invasion. When this came Blaskowitz did what he could to defend France, however, he was relieved of his command after the defeat of his forces in Lorraine. Over the following months German forces were relentlessly driven east, and Blaskowitz took over first as Commander in Chief Army Group H, The Netherlands, and then as Commander in Chief, Fortress Holland in 1945. He surrendered to the British in the Netherlands and became a prisoner of War in Nuremberg prison. He was due to stand trial as a minor war criminal, but before this took place he committed suicide on February 5, 1948. There were rumours that his death was not, in fact, suicide, but that he had actually been murdered by former SS men before he could give evidence against other German defendants.

on the Western Front where won the Pour le Mérite. By the end of the war he had reached the rank of major. Blomberg's two brothers were both killed in the conflict.

Blomberg remained in the army and in 1920 was promoted to lieutenant colonel and was appointed Chief of Staff of the Döberitz Brigade. Four years later General Hans von Seeckt appointed him as chief of army training.

In 1927 Blomberg was promoted to the rank of major general and was appointed chief of the Troop Office. In this position he clashed with Kurt von Schleicher and in 1929 was sent to East Prussia to serve under Walther von Reichenau.

In 1932 Blomberg was head of the German delegation at the Geneva Disarmament Conference. The following year Adolf Hitler appointed him minister of defence and in 1935 minister of war and commander in chief of the German Army. It was Blomberg's idea to get all soldiers to pledge an oath of personal loyalty to Hitler. In April 1936 Blomberg became Hitler's first field marshal.

Hermann Göring was jealous of Blomberg's power and used the Gestapo to obtain embarrassing information about his private life. In January, 1938, Blomberg resigned when he discovered that Göring was planning to make public the fact that his new young wife was a former prostitute.

After the Second World War Blomberg was captured by Allied troops and gave evidence at the Nuremberg War Crimes Trial. Werner Blomberg died while being held in detention on March 14, 1946.

Werner von Blomberg

Blomberg was born in Stargard, Germany, on September 2, 1878. He joined the German Army and served as a second lieutenant in the 73rd Fusilier Regiment. He attended the War Academy (1904-07) before joining the General Staff in 1908.

On the outbreak of the First World War Blomberg was General Staff Officer with the 19th Reserve Division. He served

Fedor von Bock

Another veteran of WWI who rose to prominence during the Third Reich, Fedor von Bock was born on December 3, 1880, in Kustrin, Germany. By the end of the First World War he had risen to the rank of major, and had been decorated with the coveted Pour le Mérite. His army career progressed well during the 1930s, and he played an important part in the blitzkrieg campaigns in Western Europe at the start of WWII. He was made up to field marshal in 1940 in recognition of this success, and was transferred to the eastern front where he commanded the Army Group Center. He was given the job of taking Moscow, and as this campaign got underway his forces successfully took Minsk in July 1941, and three weeks later captured Smolensk. Just as it looked as though the plan to reach Moscow might succeed, Hitler took away a large part of Bock's forces to help in the attacks on Leningrad and Kiev. By the time that Bock was able to restart the advance on Russia's capital city in October, the fierce Soviet winter was approaching, and the campaign was doomed to stall. Hitler was furious that the attack had stopped, and he replaced Bock with Gunther von Kluge. A month later Hitler changed his mind about Bock and reinstated him as commander of the Army Group South after Walther von Reichenau died in a plane crash whilst being taken home for urgent medical treatment.

Although Bock was privately appalled by the atrocities committed against civilians by the men of Heydrich's SD and Einsatzgruppen, he was unwilling to voice these thoughts to Hitler. Instead, he continued to implement the Führer's orders and pressed ahead with his campaigns against Soviet forces in

the Caucasus, and successfully took the city of Voronezh. Hitler, however, felt that his progress was too slow and dismissed him on July 15, 1942.

Bock was a prime candidate for recruitment by those who wanted to assassinate Hitler, and although he was asked to become involved by his nephew Henning von Tresckow, he declined to take part. He did, however, keep the matter to himself rather than report it to the Gestapo. As the war drew to a close, Bock volunteered himself for the interim Dönitz government after Hitler committed suicide, but before he could do so, he and his wife and daughter were killed by an Allied air raid on Hamburg on May 4, 1945.

Walther von Brauchitsch

Walther von Brauchitsch, who was born in 1881, was considered to be a highly ambitious man who was also one of the cleverest generals of the German Army. He displayed culture, charm, and professional integrity, but even though he was anti-Nazi, he became very close to the core of the party. He personally borrowed 80,000 Reichmarks from Hitler in order to finance the divorce of his first wife and the costs of remarriage.

Brauchitsch stood against the invasions of Austria and Czechoslovakia, but was not entirely unhappy with the plans for Germany to go to war. He refused to get involved when the first attempt to overthrow Hitler took place in 1938, even though he

had the power and influence to make a real contribution to it. He did, however, do his best to convince Hitler that Germany could not win a drawn-out war in Europe, but this only resulted in the Führer flying into a rage of insults and abuse. Hitler told his high command that he would defeat the West within a year, and pressed ahead with his invasion plans.

Brauchitsch organized a large part of the blitzkrieg campaign in western Europe, and did such a good job of it that Hitler awarded him and eleven other generals the field marshal's baton. The manner in which German forces drove all before them in Europe convinced Brauchitsch that they would be able to do the same in Russia. He was appointed Commander-in-Chief of

Operation "Barbarossa"—the invasion of Russia, and set about implementing Hitler's orders. These included co-signing papers known as the Commissar Order and Order for Guerrilla Warfare which allowed for the mass extermination of captured Soviet prisoners of war and civilians.

When Hitler transferred a large part of the forces which were aimed at taking Moscow, Brauchitsch was appalled as it was clear the campaign could not succeed before the winter set in. He could not face telling the Führer in person, however, and instead made his feelings known in a series of written memoranda. Unable to believe that he had personally been responsible for ruining Brauchitsch's plans to take Moscow, Hitler instead blamed him for the failure. The criticisms were so abusive that Brauchitsch suffered a heart attack, and he was relieved of command in December 1941. Hitler then took direct control of the Wehrmacht himself.

After the July 20 attempt on Hitler's life failed, Brauchitsch condemned the conspirators in a public article and praised Himmler's appointment as Commander-in-Chief of the Home Army. He also denounced some of those he thought were involved—this made him extremely unpopular with a large part of the Wehrmacht's officer corps.

When the Nuremberg Trials started after the war was over, Brauchitsch was charged with crimes against humanity and complicity. Although he denied the charges, he was unable to put up a realistic defence. Before the trial could be brought to a conclusion, however, he died in prison in 1948 as a result of ill-health.

Wilhelm Canaris

Admiral Wilhelm Canaris is one of the most interesting characters of the Third Reich era. He was born on January 1, 1887, in Aplerbeck, Germany, and earned himself a reputation as a hero during WWI when he served as a submarine captain. He was later recruited as a military spy for Germany, and he rose steadily through the ranks until he was appointed to head the Abwehr Military Intelligence in 1935.

He was against Hitler's plan to wage war, and did his best to prevent the Führer from invading Czechoslovakia—he was also personally involved in the attempts to overthrow Hitler in 1938 and 1939. After seeing SS troops murder 200 Jews in

Poland by locking them in a synagogue and setting it on fire, he risked his life to end Hitler's reign. His intelligence officers gave him countless reports of atrocities and of plans for many more, including the killings of large numbers of Polish nobility and clergy. When he tried to protest about this to the Führer, he was told by General Wilhelm Keitel, Chief of the Armed Forces High Command to keep his views to himself.

Since he could not find a way to stop the mass exterminations and other atrocities being committed, Canaris resolved to find other ways to hinder the Nazis. One of these was to ensure that detailed reports of the appalling events were smuggled out so that the wider world would find out about them. He got his intelligence agents to pass these reports on to Dr. Josef Muller, a leading figure in the Catholic resistance to Hitler, who then saw to it that they were safely transported to the Vatican.

Canaris not only tried to stop the atrocities that Reinhard Heydrich's men were committing, but he also played a major part in the army's own plans to assassinate Hitler. As part of this effort he flew to Smolensk March 1943 to help co-conspirators who were on the staff of the Army Group Center. Having done what he could there, he continued to risk his life to save others. He managed, for instance, to prevent a number of captured French officers being executed in Tunisia, as well as saving the lives of hundreds of Jews during the course of the war. Many of his achievements will probably never be known, but one those that is known about concerned seven Jews who were duc to be sent to a concentration camp. Canaris personally went to Himmler and complained that the Gestapo were arresting his agents. He was

able to take charge of them, and his men later smuggled them out of Germany.

Canaris created a secret anti-Nazi regime within the Abwehr, and recruited many enemies of the regime, turning them into Abwehr agents. In doing so, they were able to help many Jews escape from Germany, and assist the resistance in their actions. Canaris also ensured that the Allies received information about German strategy and battle plans. This included the western offensive in 1939 as well as Hitler's plan to invade Britain. He also deliberately fed information to Hitler to fool him into believing that the Allies would not land at Anzio in 1943. On top of this, he also tried to broker a peace deal with the Allies, however, President Roosevelt rejected the idea out of hand.

When the July 1944 attempt on Hitler's life failed, Canaris and many others were arrested and imprisoned by the Gestapo. He was ill-treated for a long time, and then sent to the Flossenburg concentration camp in February 1945. Through all this time he denied any involvement, and never gave away any of his fellow participants in the Resistance Movement. In the end Canaris and several others were hanged and their corpses left to rot after a mock trial by SS Obersturmbannführer Walter Huppenkothen and Sturmbannführer Otto Thorbeckwere. Two weeks later the camp was liberated by American troops.

Karl Dönitz

Dönitz is unusual in that he not only attained an extremely high rank—Grossadmiral (Admiral of the Fleet in Royal Navy terms)—in the Kriegsmarine but that he became Hitler's nominated successor .Born in Grünau bei Berlin on September 16, 1891, after school he joined the navy and served during World War I initially with the surface fleet. He was on the Breslau when it and the Goeben broke through the British Mediterranean fleet to reach Turkish waters in 1914. He continued to serve in warships until October 1916, when he joined the submarine fleet. And it was as Commander in Chief of Submarines during World War II that he would make his mark.

When the war started in 1939, Dönitz was chosen to head the U-boat arm—at that time consisting of only 50 boats, many of them shorter-range types. However, the force immediately proved successful and Dönitz would go on to develop the tactics that brought Britain to her knees. Indeed, had it not been for the fact that Britain was able to read much of the German Enigma coded transmissions Dönitz's U-boat arm could well have won the war in the west for Hitler.

In his will, Adolf Hitler chose Dönitz as his successor as German Head of State, a choice that shows how distrustful Hitler had become of Göring and Himmler in the final days of the war in Europe. Significantly, Dönitz was not to become Führer, but rather President of Germany (Reichspräsident), a post Hitler had abolished. Propaganda Minister Joseph Goebbels was to become Head of Government and Chancellor of Germany (Reichskanzler). After Hitler committed suicide on April 30,

1945, Dönitz ruled only for a few weeks, holding office through the final surrender on May 8 until his arrest by the British on May 23 at Flensburg. He devoted most of his efforts to trying to ensure that German troops surrendered to the Americans and not to the Soviets. Following the war, Dönitz went on trial as a war criminal in the Nuremberg Trials. Unlike many of the other defendants, he was not charged with crimes against humanity. However, he was charged with being involved with waging of aggressive war, conspiracy to wage aggressive war and crimes against the laws of war. Specifically, he faced charges of waging unrestricted submarine warfare and of issuing an order after the Laconia incident not to rescue survivors from ships attacked by submarine. He served ten years as prisoner number two in Spandau prison, being released on October 1, 1956. He died on December 24, 1980.

Adolf Galland

A famous fighter ace who became Germany's youngest general, Adolf Galland was born on March 19, 1911, in Westerholt, Germany. He first took to the air when he was a youngster by learning to fly gliders, and as soon as he was old enough to do so, he joined the Luftwaffe. He received his commission as a lieutenant in October 1934, and soon afterwards led a squadron of fighters in the Spanish Civil War. He took part in 280 combat missions in Spain, including the massacre of over 1,000 innocent Spanish civilians when German planes unexpectedly bombed the quiet town of Guernica.

When WWII began, Galland was given command of a ground support unit during the blitzkrieg in Poland. During this time he won the Iron Cross and was promoted to the rank of captain. He was then transferred back to a flying post for the western offensive, and in his Messerschmitt Bf109 he shot down his first three allied planes on May 12, 1940. He increased this tally to thirteen before the start of the Battle of Britain, when he became Germany's top fighter ace with a total of 57 kills.

Galland was promoted to General of the Fighter Arm after his predecessor died on November 22, 1941. As the war went on, he realized that the Luftwaffe could not continue in its current offensive format, and that it needed to change to a more defensive role. This infuriated Hitler and Hermann Göring, and after several arguments, Galland was sacked in December 1944. He was sent back to the front line, where he flew the latest jet-powered Messerschmitt Me 262. In this cutting edge plane he shot down two more Allied aircraft, which brought his overall total score to 103.

When the war ended, Galland was imprisoned for two years, and upon his release was appointed as a military adviser in Argentina. He returned to Germany in 1955 and worked as a consultant and businessman in the aerospace and airline industries. He died on March 9, 1996

Heinz Guderian

Guderian, who rose to become commander of Hitler's General Staff, was born in Kulm, Germany, on June 17, 1888. He joined the army in 1908 at the age of 20, whereupon he was commissioned in the Jägers as a communications specialist. He gained military experience during WWI after which he joined the Freikorps. He was promoted to become the Inspector of Motorized Troops in 1922, at which time he began to take a deep interest in how tanks could be used on the battlefield. His knowledge of the subject later saw him appointed as an instructor in tank warfare.

In 1930 Guderian took command of a motorized battalion where he experimented with new ways of using tanks in battle, including finding the best way for tank commanders to communicate with each other using radios. In 1934, he was promoted to become the chief of staff of the Motorized Troops Command, and in 1935, whilst still only a colonel, he took command of the 2nd Panzer Division. He was finally promoted to lieutenant general in February 1938, shortly after which he took part in the annexation of Austria.

Although Guderian was appointed to the position of Chief of Mobile Troops, he still had problems with being taken seriously by many of the old school staff officers who considered that the infantry were the key component on the battlefield. A lot of these men were relics of WWI, and did not believe that tanks were a particularly important feature of modern warfare. This attitude changed dramatically after Guderian led the incredibly successful blitzkrieg attacks through Poland in September 1939.

Although the army's drive through Poland had been such a success, Guderian added his voice to those who tried to persuade Hitler not to attack westwards into France and the Low Countries. In spite of his misgivings, Guderian obeyed the order to press ahead with the invasion. At this stage he was under the command of General Paul von Kleist, and he moved his men forward with full speed, crossing the Meuse near Sedan on May 14,, 1940. Since the infantry were struggling to keep up, Guderian was ordered to stop and wait for them, as Kleist was an old-school man who believed that ground troops were necessary for the tanks to function properly. This caused a bitter argument between the two men, and when Guderian threatened to resign, Kleist sacked him. Hitler, however, sided with Guderian, and under pressure from General Siegmund List, Kleist was obliged to return him to duty.

Once freed of Kleist's constrictions, Guderian's men reached the English Channel at Abbeville on May 21, 1940. Two days later, Boulogne was captured, but under pressure from his High Command, Hitler decided to stop the advance to allow the supply columns to catch up. Guderian was outraged, as it allowed the British Expeditionary Force to slip from his grasp and escape from Dunkirk. After the campaigns in Western Europe had come to an end, Guderian was promoted to general and took part in Operation "Barbarossa," leading the 2nd Panzer Group. His troops took Minsk and Smolensk and then moved into the Ukraine, capturing Kiev, and then moved on towards Moscow.

Guderian was surprised both by the ferocity of the Soviet defence and the Russian winter, and consequently argued with Hitler about the tactical methods being used. After further arguments with General Fedor von Bock and General Gunther von Kluge, Guderian was sacked on December 25, 1941.

More than a year later, Hitler decided to recall Guderian, and on March 1, 1943, he was appointed to become commander of Germany's Armored Troops. By this stage the Germans no longer had the edge over the competition, and it was not long before his tanks suffered massive losses at Kursk in the biggest tank battle in history. Guderian was promoted again on July 21, 1944, when he became commander of the General Staff. After the July attempt on Hitler's life, Guderian then became an instrumental part of the fanatical purge of the German military, sitting in judgement of hundreds of officers in the Army Court of Honor. In spite of this, he continued to question Hitler's strategic decisions, and was again dismissed from office on March 28, 1945. Guderian was captured by the Americans in May 1945, but despite claims from the Polish and Russian governments that he was a war criminal, he was released in 1948, and died on May 17, 1954.

Franz Halder

Born in 1884 in Germany, Franz Halder b rose to become Commander in Chief of the German Army before falling from grace and being arrested by the Gestapo. He served in the army in WWI as one of the Crown Prince of Bavaria's staff. When the Nazis came to power he worked his way up until he was appointed as Chief of General Staff in 1938, replacing General Ludwig Beck.

Although Halder did much of the organizational work for the invasion of Poland, he was not in favor of the attack on France and the Low Countries. He was involved in the 1938 and 1939 plots to overthrow Hitler, however, was too weak to bring himself to do much more than pay lip-service to the attempts. He blamed the British Prime Minister, Chamberlain, for giving in to Hitler— he believed that had this not happened, the plot could have succeeded. Instead, it raised Hitler's popularity among both the military and the public, making an overthrow attempt much more difficult. Halder was so angry at Hitler's intention to launch the Western Offensive that he even went to see the Führer on several occasions with a pistol in his pocket. Each time he tried, however, his nerve failed him, and he was unable to carry out the killing.

In opposing the western offensive, he marked himself in Hitler's eyes as yet another one of the army's dissenters. In spite of this, his planning expertise was used for the campaign, as well as for Operation "Sea Lion" (which was later abandoned) and for Operation "Barbarossa." When Walther von Brauchitsch resigned as Commander in Chief of the German Army, Halder was appointed as his successor. It was not long before disagreements

with Hitler caused him to fall from grace, and he was replaced by General Kurt Zeitzler in September 1942.

When the July 1944 assassination plot failed, Hitler initiated a massive witch-hunt to root out any possible co-conspirators. During this episode Halder was arrested and imprisoned in Dachau Concentration Camp. He was fortunate that the advancing American army liberated the camp before the Gestapo had a chance to execute him. After the war was over, Halder took part in the Nuremberg War Crimes Trial as a witness against several prominent Nazi Party members. Franz Halder died in 1972.

Erich Höpner

Höpner was another leading German Army officer who became involved in the plots to kill Hitler. He was born in Frankfurt Germany on September 14, 1886, and served in the army in WWI. After the war ended, he joined the Freikorps whilst remaining in the army. By 1938 he had risen to the level of Major General, commanding the 1st Light Division of Panzers. When the 1938 coup attempt was being planned, he placed his tank unit at the disposal of the conspirators—in the end though, this attempt never went ahead.

He was involved in the invasions of Czechoslovakia and Poland, and then in March 1939, he replaced Heinz Guderian as commander of XVI Army Corps. When the western campaign through France and the Low Countries began, he led his troops through Belgium and helped push the British Expeditionary Force back to Dunkirk. His successes during this time were widely acclaimed.

In Operation "Barbarossa" he commanded the Fourth Panzer Army, which took part in the attack on Leningrad. After this they were moved over to the Army Group Center under the command of Gunther von Kluge for the ill-fated advance on Moscow. Höpner's troops managed to get within 20 miles of Russia's capital city by December 5, 1941, but when the Red Army's massive counter-attack began, he pulled them back to avoid their total destruction. Hitler was outraged by this, and Höpner was unceremoniously sacked from his post. Several other senior officers stood up for him, and Hitler eventually allowed him to retire with his full pension.

Höpner was later persuaded to join the 1944 plot to assassinate Hitler, and when it failed he was quickly arrested by the Gestapo. He was tried and found guilty of treason, before being hanged at Ploetzwnsee Prison on August 8, 1944.

Hermann Hoth

The son of an army medical officer, Hermann Hoth was born in Neuruppin, Germany, on April 12, 1885, and joined the German Army in 1904, and commissioned as a lieutenant in 1905. He was promoted to captain in 1914, and assigned to the General Staff of Army High Command the same year. He served in many different positions during WWI, most of which were attached to the High Command or General Staff.

After the war ended he stayed in the army and rose through various infantry and artillery units to become commanding officer of the 18th Division at Liegnitz, in 1935. He was promoted again on November 10, 1938, when he was made up to lieutenant general and given command of the 15th Motorized Corps. When Hitler began the expansion of Germany, Hoth took part in the invasion of Poland, as well as in the western offensive where he led his troops through the Ardennes and up to the English Channel coast. After this he moved his men further west through Normandy and Brittany. His successful leadership during this period was rewarded with promotion to general on July 19, 1940.

When Operation "Barbarossa" began he commanded Panzer Group 3, and succeeded in capturing both Minsk and Vitebsk before taking his troops towards Moscow. In October 1941, he was given command of the Seventeenth Army in the Ukraine, but his men were driven back by the Red Army in January 1942. Hoth was appointed as Höpner's replacement in June 1942, taking command of the Fourth Panzer Army. In this role he took part in the siege of Stalingrad, and then later he was involved in the tank battle at Kursk in July 1943. Hitler was infuriated that

Hoth withdrew his men to better defensive positions during the battle, and finally recalled him to Germany in November 1943, where he spent the rest of the war in the reserve forces.

He was imprisoned by the Allies at the end of the war, and faced charges of war crimes at the Nuremberg Trials. He was found guilty and was sentenced to 15 years in prison on October 27, 1948. After six years he was released, and spent a quiet retirement writing about military history; he died in 1971.

Alfred Jodl

Jodl was born in Würzburg, Germany, on May 10, 1890. He attended cadet school and 1910 joined a field military regiment in the German Army.

Soon after the outbreak of the First World War Jodl suffered a severe thigh wound. He recovered and saw further action on the Western Front and the Eastern Front. Disillusioned by Germany's defeat he considered leaving the army and becoming a doctor.

In 1935 Jodl was promoted to the rank of general major. After the Anschluss he was sent to Vienna as head of the 44th Artillery Command. He returned to Germany and in September he took part in the invasion of Poland.

A strong supporter of the National Socialist German Workers Party (NSDAP), Jodl worked closely with Adolf Hitler and in October, 1939, was appointed chief of operations. In January, 1944, Jodl was promoted to the rank of Generaloberst.

Jodl came close to be killed when the bomb exploded in the July Plot. He recovered and in May, 1945, signed the unconditional surrender of Germany to the Allies. Soon afterwards he was arrested and charged with war crimes.

At the Nuremberg War Crimes Trial Jodl was charged of approving orders that violated the rules of war. Alfred Jodl was found guilty and hanged on October 16, 1946.

Wilhelm Keitel

The son of a landowner, Wilhelm Keitel was born in Hanover on September 22, 1882. He joined the German Army and in 1902 became a second lieutenant in the 46th Field Artillery.

Keitel had reached the rank of captain by the outbreak of the First World War. In September 1914 Keitel was seriously wounded by a shell splinter. After returning to duty he became a battery commander before being appointed to the General Staff in March 1915. He also served as an officer with XIX Reserve Corps (1916-17) and the 199th Infantry Division (1917) before returning to the General Staff in Berlin in December 1917.

After the war Keitel was a member of the right-wing terrorist Freikorps group and served on the frontier with Poland in 1919. He remained in the army and spent three years as an instructor at the School of Cavalry at Hanover (1920-23). This was followed by a spell with the 6th Artillery Regiment.

Assigned to the Troop Office he was promoted to lieutenant colonel in February 1929. Later that year he became head of the Organizations Department. In this role he was involved in secret preparations to triple the size of the German Army.

In January 1933, Adolf Hitler gained power and immediately Keitel's old friend, Werner von Blomberg, was appointed Minister of Defence. Soon afterwards Blomberg introduced him to Hitler. Keitel was impressed and became a devoted supporter of the new leader.

In February 1938 Keitel became Commander-in-Chief of the High Command of the Armed Forces (OKW). He now arranged to have his friend, Heinrich von Brauchitsch, appointed as

Commander-in-Chief of the Army.

During the Second World War Keitel, Alfred Jodl and Walther Warlimont were the most important figures in the OKW. He was a loyal supporter of Hitler's policies and after the invasion of Poland he issued orders to the Schutz Staffeinel (SS) and the Gestapo to exterminate the country's Jews.

Keitel advised against the Western Offensive and Operation "Barbarossa" but quickly backed down when Hitler responded aggressively. Both times he tried to resign but Hitler refused him permission to go.

In May 1941 Keitel signed the Commissar Order which instructed German field commanders to execute Communist Party officials immediately they were captured. In July 1941 he signed another order giving Heinrich Himmler the power to implement his racial program in the Soviet Union.

In September 1942 Keitel and Alfred Jodl defended Field Marshal Wilhelm List against the criticisms of Adolf Hitler. This resulted in Jodl being sacked and for many months afterwards Hitler refused to shake hands with Keitel. This was the last time that Keitel was to challenge Hitler's military decisions. He was now referred to by other officers as "Lakaitel" (the nodding ass).

Over the next two years Keitel issued orders for the execution of striking workers, the extermination of Jews and the killing of captured partisans. He also suggested that German civilians should be encouraged to lynch captured Allied airman.

After the war Keitel was arrested and tried at Nuremberg as a major war criminal. In court his main defence was that he was merely obeying orders claiming that he was "never permitted to make decisions". Found guilty he was executed on October 16, 1946. His autobiography, In Service of the Reich, was published after his death.

Albert Kesselring

Kesselring, the son of school teacher, was born in Bayreuth, Germany, on August 8, 1881. He joined the German Army in 1904 and became an officer cadet in the 2nd Bavarian Foot Artillery Regiment at Metz.

During the First World War Kesselring was transferred to the German Army Air Service where he trained as a balloon observer. While in this post he developed a close friendship with Hermann Göring.

Kesselring remained in the armed forces and was promoted to major general in 1932. The following year he joined the recently established Luftwaffe where he served under Erhard Milch. In June 1936, despite the objections of Milch, Göring appointed Kesselring as the organization's chief of staff.

On the outbreak of the Second World War Kesselring became commander of First Air Fleet and provided air support to General Fedor von Bock and Army Group North in the invasion of Poland. The following year he moved to the Second Air Fleet and supported the infantry in the invasions of Belgium, Holland and France. Despite criticisms for his performance during the Dunkirk evacuations, Kesselring was made a field marshal on July 19, 1940.

Kesselring remained in North Africa where he supported General Erwin Rommel in the Desert War. On November 10, 1942, Kesselring was appointed to serve under Benito Mussolini as deputy commander of Italian forces. In this position he was unable to prevent the loss of Tunisia and Sicily.

In the winter of 1943 Kesselring withdrew his forces to what became known as the Gustav Line on the Italian peninsula south of Rome. Organized along the Garigliano and Rapido rivers it included Monte Cassino, a hilltop site of a sixth-century Benedictine monastery. Defended by 15 German divisions the line was fortified with gun pits, concrete bunkers, turreted machine-gun emplacements, barbed-wire and minefields.

On October 25, 1944, Kesselring was seriously injured when his car collided with a gun coming out of a side road. He was in hospital for three months and his command in Italy was taken over by General Heinrich Vietinghoff. When he recovered Adolf Hitler named Kesselring as supreme commander in the south of the country.

Kesselring, the only one of the early field marshals not to be sacked by Hitler, was taken prisoner on May 6, 1945. Tried as a war criminal he was found guilty on May 6, 1947 and condemned to death. Soon afterwards this sentence was commuted to life in prison and was released for health reasons in October 1952. The following year he published his autobiography, A Soldier to the Last Day (1953). Albert Kesselring died on July 16, 1960.

Paul von Kleist

Born on August 8, 1881, in Hessen, Germany, von Kleist's father was a mathematics teacher who encouraged him to join the army, which he did in 1900. In 1901, he was commissioned into the 3rd Royal Field Artillery Regiment as a second lieutenant, and then went on to study for a year at the cavalry school in Hanover in 1908. In 1910 he was accepted into the Berlin War Academy which he attended for two years. When WWI started, he had risen to the rank of Rittmeister, or captain of cavalry, of the 1st Prince's Own Hussar Regiment. He led a cavalry squadron on the Eastern Front at Tannenberg in 1914. After this he was raised to the rank of staff officer, and transferred to the 85th Infantry Division, which was also on the Russian front. In 1917, he was made Chief of Staff of the Guards Cavalry Division. When the Russians signed the Brest-Litovsk Treaty in 1918, Kleist was posted to the Western Front. He remained in the army after the war ended, serving in various cavalry units until being made Chief of Staff of Wehrkreis III in 1928.

In 1932 he was promoted to the rank of major general, and then again in August 1936 to general of cavalry. In this position he organized the military expansion in Silesia, however, his anti-Nazi views were known, and he was forced into retirement by General Heinrich von Brauchitsch in February 1938. This did not last long, however, and when the war started, he was recalled to command the XXII Corps under General Siegmund List during the invasion of Poland. Kleist successfully captured the oilfields near Lvov, and then joined up with General Heinz Guderian at the Bug River on September 17, 1939. His clear military abilities saw him being promoted again on February 29, 1940, this time to commander of the Panzer forces in the Western Offensive. On May 9, 1940, Kleist led his armored troops through the forests of the Ardennes in a slow but certain manner. Meanwhile, General Heinz Guderian led his tanks across Meuse at great speed, which caused Kleist great concern. He felt that the Panzer needed infantry back-up, and so ordered Guderian to stop and allow the ground troops of General Siegmund List's Twelfth Army to catch up. After a bitter disagreement, Kleist sacked Guderian. Hitler was not happy about this, however, and intervened on Guderian's behalf. He ordered General List to persuade Kleist to reinstate him, and Guderian's troops reached the English Channel at

Abbeville on May 21, 1940.

Kleist was sent to invade Bulgaria in July 1940 as commander of the 1st Panzer Group, and then in Operation "Barbarossa" he led 14 divisions, five of which were panzer units. He led his men in a very successful campaign through the Ukraine where he wiped out nearly 20 divisions of Soviet troops. He then turned north and joined Heinz Guderian at Kiev. On November 20, 1941, his men entered Rostov. He was not able to hold this position, however, and facing overwhelming odds from the Red Army combined with the bitter Russian winter, he had to withdraw his troops. In the summer of 1942 he was able to push into Russian territory again, reaching well into the Caucasus. When winter returned, however, he had to withdraw for a second time.

When the Red Army struck back with a massive counter-offensive in March 1944, Kleist—who was by now head of Army Group A, was unable to hold them back. Hitler was infuriated, and on March 29, 1944, called both Kleist and General Erich von Manstein back to Germany where he sacked them. Later that year he was arrested as a possible conspirator in the plot to assassinate Hitler, however, the Gestapo were unable to link him to any evidence, and so he was released. When the Allies arrived at the end of the war he was arrested and handed over to Marshall Tito in Yugoslavia where he was sentenced to 15 years for war crimes. In 1948, he was extradited to the Soviet Union and sent to the Wladimir Prison Camp where he died in 1954.

Günther von Kluge

Kluge, who was born in Germany in 1882, became one of the major conspirators in the plot to assassinate Hitler. He was educated at the Military Academy, and then served on the army's General Staff from 1910 to 1918. After WWI ended, he rose through the ranks to become a colonel in 1930, a major-general in 1933, and a lieutenant-general in 1934. Two years later he was put in command of an army corps where his skill with leading mobile troops was noticed by Hitler.

Kluge himself was an anti-Nazi who hated the persecution of the Jews, and believed that Hitler's aggressive foreign policies would be the ruin of Germany. He did, however, have deep-seated resentment at the Versailles Treaty's handing over of West Prussia to Poland, and so was very much in favor of reclaiming these territories. Kluge demonstrated outstanding leadership in the invasion of Poland, and won Hitler's admiration for his efforts. He was appalled, however, at the atrocities committed by Heydrich's Einsatzgruppen forces, although he was unable to do anything constructive to stop them. Kluge was shocked that Hitler intended to wage war in Western Europe, and was tempted to join the conspiracy against the Führer. In the end he decided against doing so, as he believed that Hitler was still too popular for this to work.

When the western offensive against France and the Low Countries began, Kluge once again displayed his superb military leadership of Panzer divisions. During this time he worked with General Erwin Rommel, and grew close to him. Kluge was awarded the field marshal's baton by Hitler in June 1941 for his achievements, and appointed to be one of the leading generals for Operation "Barbarossa". For this he was moved to the Army Group Center under Field Marshal Feodor von Bock. Kluge was one of many army officers who strongly disagreed with Hitler's plans to move a large part of the Army Group Center's Panzer forces away from their intended target of Moscow to assist in taking Leningrad and the eastern Ukraine. When the ill-fated troops attempted to complete their task, they were not strong enough to take the capital city and were beaten back. Hitler would not allow the troops to be withdrawn to safety, and these angry denials left Kluge with strong misgivings about the Führer's future.

When Feodor von Bock was taken ill in July 1942, Kluge was appointed by Hitler to take over his command as Commander-in-Chief of Army Group Center. At the group's headquarters in Smolensk, Kluge became good friends with his Chief of Staff, Colonel Henning von Tresckow—a man who by then was already leading the plot against Hitler. Tresckow did not find it hard to convince Kluge that the Führer was a madman who would lead Germany to total destruction. The other officers were all co-conspirators, and together they persuaded Kluge that Hitler had to be eliminated. The plan was to kill Hitler by inviting him to Smolensk and then shooting him at the dinner table. Kluge forbade the bid as he felt it was an ungentlemanly way to behave. This way they lost what was probably the best chance they had to kill Hitler.

When Hitler lost faith in Field Marshal Gerd von Rundstedt on June 29, 1944, he appointed Kluge as his replacement as Commander-in-Chief West. After spending time with Hitler, Kluge decided that the Führer was the only person able to save Germany, but on returning to Rommel's headquarters at La Roche-Guyon, he was embroiled in a bitter argument. In the end Rommel managed to persuade Kluge that he ought to see for himself how bad things were at the western front, which he did shortly afterwards. When he returned, Kluge was convinced that Rommel and the other were right, and that either Hitler had to be removed or that Germany had to sue for peace. Kluge, however, when told about the latest plot only agreed to be involved if they succeeded in killing Hitler. When the plot failed, the conspirators led by Stülpnagel begged Kluge to command the armies in France to come to their aid, or at the very least surrender to the Allies. Kluge would not answer them, and when pressed by Stülpnagel he threatened to have him arrested. As a result the coup attempt collapsed, and Hitler survived to continue the war.

When the Allies began their breakout from Normandy, Kluge did his best to get Hitler to pull the army back to the Rhine to create a strong defensive line. Hitler, however, would not agree to giving up any territory at all. Kluge was severely depressed by this, and seriously contemplated surrendering to the Allies. On August 15, 1944, Hitler was told of an American radio intercept that gave him cause to believe that Kluge might have been trying to negotiate an armistice. It appears that this may well have been the case, however, Kluge had been unable to contact the Allied commanders and gave up. Hitler did not believe Kluge's explanations for his actions and sacked him. On the way back to Germany, Kluge committed suicide, convinced that he had been implicated in the July 20 assassination plot.

Erich von Manstein

Erich von Manstein, who was born in 1885, came from a long line of old-school Prussian military officers. He was brought up to believe in the tenets of chivalry and honor, and was said to have displayed great strength of character, including the ability to stand up to Hitler when he thought he was wrong. Manstein was an anti-Nazi who, like many others believed that Germany had

a right to rebuild her armies and to reclaim the lands taken from her by the Versailles Treaty. He was a strong advocate of blitzkrieg warfare, and in the western offensive of 1940 his troops were the first the cross the Seine.

During Operation "Barbarossa" he was part of the Army Group South, and planned the Crimean campaign, including the capture of Sevastopol. Hitler was so pleased with his leadership of the offensive that he rewarded Manstein with the field marshal's baton. He was moved to the Army Group North in August 1942, in an attempt to help the failed bid to capture Leningrad. He grew very frustrated with Hitler's interference in the military campaigns, and felt that the Führer's grasp of strategy was overly influenced by the wrong objectives, such as securing oilfields rather than important military targets. Manstein repeatedly argued with Hitler over the way the Russian campaign was being waged, and begged for the troops to be allowed to retreat to give them a chance to regroup.

The conspirators who were trying to overthrow Hitler tried to recruit Manstein to their cause, but he refused to join them as he believed that this was not necessary. In his eyes all that had to be done was to persuade the Führer to hand over command of the war effort to the army. Manstein, however, never betrayed the conspirators, not blamed them during his trial at Nuremberg. He was later also tried by a British military court after the Soviets made charges against him for war crimes. Although he received an 18-year sentence, he was released in 1953 after four years. He later became a senior advisor to the German government, helping them to rebuild the German army.

Erhard Milch

Erhard Milch, who was born in Wilhelmshaven, Germany on March 30, 1892, rose to become director of air armament, one of the most important positions in the German air forces. Although his later career was associated with aircraft, he started out by joining the army and serving as an artillery officer. During WWI he initially fought on the Western Front before being moved to the German Army Air Service. In this fledgling unit he was trained as an aerial observer before being promoted to the rank of captain and taking over command of Flight Squadron 6 in October 1918.

Milch stayed in the army until 1921, when he left the military

and worked for the Junkers company in the aviation industry. In 1926 he became a director of Deutsche Lufthansa, the national airline. During this time he started working secretly with Hermann Göring to create the Luftwaffe, something that was forbidden by the Versailles Treaty. After the Nazis came to power Milch was appointed as Göring's deputy as State Secretary in the Reich Air Ministry, a position that oversaw the production of armaments.

When the purge of Jews began, Milch was in a difficult situation—rumours suggested that his father was Jewish, which resulted in an investigation by the Gestapo. In the end his mother signed a legal affidavit which stated that her husband was not Milch's real father—this was enough for him to be declared an Aryan. After this temporary glitch, his career continued to prosper; in 1938 he was promoted to colonel general, and in 1939 he took over command of Luftflotte V during the Norwegian offensive. He was successfully involved in the western campaign through France and the Low Countries, after which he was promoted to field marshal. In 1941, he was again promoted, this time to the position of Air Inspector General.

When the Luftwaffe failed to perform well in the Soviet campaigns, it was clear that Hermann Göring had lost his grip on his command of the Luftwaffe. In order to try and remedy the situation, both Milch and Joseph Goebbels tried to persuade Hitler to replace him. The Führer was not convinced, and refused to do so. In the end it was Göring who forced Milch to resign as director of air armament in June 1944. After this he served under Albert Speer until Hitler committed suicide, when he tried to flee to the Baltic Coast. He was arrested on May 4, 1945, and sent to the Nuremberg Trials to face charges of war crimes. He was found guilty and although he was sentenced to life imprisonment, he was released in June 1954. Erhard Milch died at Wuppertal-Barmen on January 25, 1972.

Walther Model

Model became a fanatical Nazi and one of the Third Reich's top military commanders. He was born in Genthin, Germany, on January 24, 1891, the son of a musician. He joined the army and distinguished himself during WWI by winning both First and Second Class Iron Crosses. He stayed in the army after the war ended and rose through the ranks until in 1930, he was promoted to become head of the technical warfare section at the war ministry.

Model took part in the invasion of Poland in 1939, and then in 1940, he was moved to the Sixteenth Army for the offensive in Western Europe under the command of Ernst Busch. For Operation "Barbarossa" he served under Heinz Guderian, and in October 1941 he was appointed to command XXXXI Panzer Corps. He was posted to the Ninth Army on January 14, 1942, where he had a heated argument with Hitler over his requirement for a panzer corps to support his troops against the Russian partisans. Although the Führer refused, Model was not cowed and told him that since he was at the front line he was in a better position to judge what was needed. In the end Hitler acquiesced and the extra troops Model wanted were provided. In spite of his troubles with the Führer, he was promoted to general in February 1942.

When the Red Army began to push the Germans back out of the Soviet Union in 1943, Model ensured that the towns they left behind were totally destroyed and many civilians massacred. These activities saw Model later being classed as a war criminal. When Hitler tired of Erich von Manstein's inability to defeat the Soviets in March 1944, he replaced him as Commander in Chief in the Soviet Union with Walther Model. Later that summer he was moved across to the Western Front as the replacement for Günther von Kluge, but after 18 days Hitler decided to give the job to Gerd von Rundstedt instead. After losing this new post, he was transferred to command the Army Group B in Holland and Belgium. While there he did an excellent job of holding the Allies back. When Hitler launched his last-ditch strike back in October 1944, Model led his forces against the Allies in the Ardennes Offensive. After this failed, the German armies were in ruins, and in early 1945, Model withdrew to defend the industrial areas in the Ruhr. He continued to argue with Hitler, however, especially when he was not allowed to withdraw his men to better positions.

When the end of the war came he realized that he would be tried as a war criminal, and rather than face this fate, Walther Model committed suicide on April 21, 1945.

Friedrich Paulus

Born in Breitenau, Germany, on September 23, 1890, Friedrich Paulus rose to become one of Hitler's key field marshals. Although he was a talented man, he lacked the necessary breeding to be accepted by the aristocratic officers of the German Navy. He studied law for a while, but then joined the army in 1910. In 1911 he was commissioned as a second lieutenant in the 3rd Baden Infantry Regiment. He served throughout WWI on both the Western and Eastern Fronts, and when the war ended, he stayed in the army and became adjutant to the 14th Infantry Regiment at Konstanz. He served as a staff officer in several different roles during the 1920s, where he was said to be "slow, but very methodical", but that he "lacked decisiveness".

As the Third Reich continued to establish itself, Paulus continued to get promoted. In 1934, he was made up to lieutenant colonel, and appointed to become commander of Motor Transport Section 3. The next year he replaced Heinz Guderian as chief of staff to the commander of Germany's Mechanized Forces, and then was promoted to major general in 1939. His rise continued just before war broke out when he was made chief of staff of the Tenth Army. He took part in both the invasion of Poland and the Western Offensive through France and the Low Countries, and then in June 1940, he was promoted again, this time to lieutenant general. A few weeks later he was appointed to the position of deputy chief of the General Staff. When he visited North Africa to review Rommel and the Deutsches Afrika Korps, Paulus was highly critical of this highly acclaimed officer.

Paulus made many recommendations as to how Operation "Barbarossa" should be carried out, and in December 1941 Field Marshal Walther von Reichenau suggested to Hitler that Paulus should be given command of the Sixth Army. The Führer accepted the idea, and Paulus was promoted to general before starting his new role on January 1, 1942. He met with stiff resistance from the Red Army and his men had to pull back to defensive positions. On May 9, 1942, the Sixth Army was attacked at Volchansk by General Semen Timoshenko, who was in charge of 640,000 men. Paulus was heavily outnumbered, and he moved his men back until General Paul von Kleist was able to send the First Panzer Army to his rescue. Paulus then launched a highly successful counter-attack which earned him the Knight's Cross.

Paulus was then ordered to move on Stalingrad with 250,000 men, 500 tanks, 7,000 guns and mortars, and 25,000 horses. He was not able to move his forces as quickly as he would have liked due to a fuel shortage. When his men eventually reached Stalingrad, they surrounded the city while the Luftwaffe bombed it relentlessly. When the troops went in they had to fight for every house, and took enormous casualties. As they fought their way from street to street, Hitler ordered Paulus to take the city at whatever cost. By October 4, Paulus had lost 40,000 men and desperately begged Hitler for reinforcements. When these arrived,

Stalin also put more men into the battle. To make matters worse, the weather turned the area into a vast sea of mud, making it almost impossible for further supplies to be delivered.

Although Paulus did his best to launch further attacks, the Soviets fought back every time, and in the end the Germans took such heavy casualties that Paulus was forced to pull back. When Hitler heard about this he ordered Paulus to hold his ground and not retreat any further as Göring had promised that the Luftwaffe would be able to provide all the supplies that were needed by air. Although Paulus realized that it was going to prove almost impossible to achieve, he told his officers that they must obey the Führer's orders. The airlift proved to be a total failure, but rather than allow Paulus to stage a breakout, Hitler tried to get Erich von Manstein's Fourth Panzer Army to rescue them. This was also abortive, and Paulus told Manstein that his men were too weak to break out of the city. Hitler was determined that Paulus should not surrender, and in order to give him reason to hold out, he promoted Paulus to field marshal on January 30, 1943, telling him that no German field marshal had ever been taken prisoner. Instead of committing suicide as the Führer wanted, he surrendered to the Red Army the next day. The attempt to take Stalingrad cost the German Army 150,000 dead and a further 91,000 were taken prisoner; of these only around 7,000 survived until the end of the war.

After being taken prisoner, Paulus was told of the execution of his friends Erich Höpner and Erwin von Witzleben for their part in the July plot. This news shocked Paulus, and caused him to agree to help the Soviets. As a result he began to make anti-Nazi broadcasts on the radio calling for German soldiers to desert. Hitler was enraged by this behaviour, and ordered that Paulus's family be rounded up and imprisoned. Paulus appeared at the Nuremberg Trials as a witness for the prosecution in 1946. He was released from a Russian prison in 1953, whereupon he settled in Dresden and worked as an inspector of the German police. He died of cancer in 1957.

Erich Räder

Erich Räder, the son of a headmaster, was born in Wandsbek, Schleswig-Holstein, on April 24, 1876. After a good classical education he entered the Imperial Navy in 1894. He made rapid progress and became Chief of Staff to Franz von Hipper in 1912. During the First World War he saw action and in 1928 was promoted to admiral and head of the German Navy.

Räder disliked the domestic policies of the National Socialist German Workers Party (NSDAP) but supported Adolf Hitler in his attempts to restore Germany as a great power. In 1939 Hitler promoted Räder to the rank of grand admiral, the first German to hold this post since Alfred von Tirpitz.

Räder strategy was to build a German Navy that could

challenge the British Navy. This brought him into conflict with Hermann Göring who as director of the German economy directed more resources to the Luftwaffe than the navy.

In October 1939 Räder sent Adolf Hitler a proposal for capturing Denmark and Norway. He argued that Germany would not be able to defeat Britain unless it created naval bases in these countries. In April 1940 Hitler gave permission for this move but he was disappointed by the heavy losses that the German Navy suffered during the achievement of this objective.

Räder supported Operation "Sealion," the planned German invasion of Britain, but argued that first the Luftwaffe had to gain air superiority. When Hermann Göring failed to win the Battle of Britain Reader advised Hitler to call off the invasion. He was also a strong opponent of Operation "Barbarossa".

Adolf Hitler grew increasingly disillusioned with the performance of the German Navy and after the Lützow and Admiral Hipper failed to stop a large Arctic convoy he accused his commander of incompetence. Räder resigned in January, 1943 and was replaced by Karl Dönitz as Commander in Chief of the navy.

At the Nuremberg War Crimes Trial Räder was found guilty of conspiring to wage aggressive war and was sentenced to life imprisonment. He was released in 1955 and in retirement wrote his memoirs Mein Leben (1957). Erich Räder died in Kiel, on November 6, 1960.

Walter von Reichenau

Born in Germany on August 16, 1884, Walter von Reichenau became one of Hitler's key generals. He was the son of a Prussian general, and so it was natural for him to join the army after he finished his education at the age of eighteen. He was commissioned as an officer at the age of 20 in the 1st Guards Field Artillery Regiment. Just before WWI began, he was sent to the War Academy in Berlin for General Staff training, but when the war started he was transferred to the Western Front. During his time at the front he won the Iron Cross, and was promoted to captain before the war ended. He stayed in the army after hostilities ceased, and served on the General Staff with the Wehrkreis. He continued to rise through the ranks, and in

February 1931 he was appointed to the position of Chief of Staff of Wehrkreis I in East Prussia.

In 1932, Reichenau was introduced to Hitler by his uncle, who was a fervent Nazi Party member. This had a bid effect on him, and he joined the party straight away. When Hitler came to power in 1933, Reichenau was appointed as head of the Ministerial Office of the Reichswehr Ministry. This made him the key link between the Nazi Party and the German Army. At this stage, he and Werner von Blomberg were getting increasingly worried by the power of the Sturm Abteilung (SA). The SA's leader, Ernst Röhm, was a particular concern to them as he was trying to gain more control over the military. Reichenau believed that Röhm could well be plotting a coup to overthrow Hitler, so he conspired with Hermann Göring and Heinrich Himmler to see Röhm and the SA fall from grace. This bid was successful, and Hitler authorized the arrest of all the leading SA members, many of whom were murdered.

Reichenau was promoted to lieutenant general in August 1935 and appointed to become commander of the Wehrkreis VII in Munich. In 1936, he was appointed general of artillery and in 1938 he replaced Brauchitsch as Commander-in-Chief of Army Corps 4. During the invasion of Poland in September 1939, Reichenau led the Tenth Army, and then in 1940 he led the Sixth Army through France and the Low Countries. Hitler promoted him to field marshal on July 19, 1940, and although he was against the plan to invade Russia, he led the Sixth Army, capturing Kiev, Belgorod, Kharkov and Kursk. During this time his men committed many atrocities against the Jews with Reichenau's full consent.

Reichenau was a keep fit fanatic, and he ran many miles every day, even in the extreme cold of the Russian winter. On January 12, 1942, he collapsed with a major heart attack after a particularly gruelling run. When he had still not regained consciousness after five days, he was flown back to Germany. On January 17, 1942, the plane he was on crash-landed, and he was killed.

Erwin Rommel

Erwin Rommel, who as the "Desert Fox," became one of the most famous and respected officers in military history, was born on November 15, 1891, at Heidenheim, Germany. He quickly earned himself a reputation for bravery and cunning on the battlefields of WWI, where within a few months he won the Iron Cross Second Class. Later in the war, with only a handful of men at his side, he captured 9,000 Italian soldiers and 150 officers, along with 81 field guns. For this achievement he was awarded the Pour le Mérite—this was a great honor, for he was only a captain at the time, and the award was normally only given to senior generals. After the war ended he stayed in the army, but was not promoted again until 1933, when he was raised to the rank of major. He then went on to teach at the War College, where he was promoted to colonel in 1937.

Although Rommel had little interest in politics, he was very much in favor of regaining the lands and rights taken from Germany in the Versailles Treaty. When Hitler started to surreptitiously restore the country's military strength, Rommel was full of admiration, and began a close working relationship with the Führer. When Hitler entered the Sudetenland in October 1938, and Prague in March 1939, Rommel was at his side. As the Nazi Party's power rose, however, Rommel's dislike for the regime grew.

When the Western Offensive through France and the Low Countries began, Rommel demonstrated an ability to move his men and equipment at great speed, and always led them from the front. During this campaign he once covered 150 miles in a single day, and over the six weeks it lasted he captured almost 100,000 French troops and 450 tanks with losses of only 42 tanks. When the offensive was over, he returned to Germany a hero and was promoted to the rank of lieutenant general.

It was in the North African desert campaign, however, that Rommel really gained his reputation as a master of the battlefield. His superb leadership and ability to "think on his feet" consistently outwitted the ponderous Allied chain of command. He convincingly defeated the British Eighth Army at Tobruk in June 1942, and in the process destroyed more than 260 tanks and took 30,000 prisoners. He was promoted to Field Marshal when he was only 49, which made him the youngest in the German Army. While the strength of the Allies in North Africa continued to grow, Rommel's forces were dwindling rapidly. It was clear that before long he would not have enough men and equipment to continue the fight, so he pleaded with Hitler to permit the evacuation of the Afrika Korps back to Europe.

When the Führer repeatedly refused to listen to reason, Rommel lost all faith in him, questioning his sanity and his

right to lead Germany. Although he was low on fuel, troops and equipment, Rommel did his best to outwit the Allies, and scored many successes as he out-ran the pursuing enemy. In the end, however, there was no way that Rommel could sustain his army without supplies, and he returned to Germany before his men were forced to capitulate.

After the North African campaign had come to its disastrous end, Rommel was sent to France to try and ensure that the coastal defences were strong enough to repel the expected Allied invasion. He threw himself into the task at hand, but realized that there was no way that they would be able to properly defend such an extensive coastline. He and Field Marshal Gerd von Rundstedt tried to persuade Hitler to agree to the German Army withdrawing to a more easily defended line, but once again this was only met with angry tirades. By this time Rommel could see that Hitler was prepared to see Germany entirely destroyed rather than give way to reason.

Rommel's attitude towards Hitler was not lost on the coup conspirators, and they desperately sought to recruit him to their cause. The leader of the plot, Colonel Claus von Stauffenberg, arranged for General Karl-Heinrich von Stülpnagel—the military governor of Paris to invite Rommel to Paris for secret talks. After much discussion, Rommel agreed to pledge his support for the cause if Hitler did not respond to one last message warning of the dire state of the German situation. This was given to Günther von Kluge for immediate delivery, however, it was not passed on for two weeks. In the meantime—on July 17, 1944, Rommel was severely injured when his car crashed after being strafed by RAF fighters. This meant that he was unable to help the conspirators when Stauffenberg's bomb failed to kill Hitler three days later.

It was inevitable that Rommel would be implicated, and in the end he was offered the chance to commit suicide and receive a burial with full military honors, or to be tried for high treason. The latter would create severe problems for his family, and so he agreed to take the proffered cyanide capsule after saying goodbye to his wife and son. He died on October 14, 1944, and was buried as a national hero with full honors.

Gerd von Rundstedt

Gerd von Rundstedt, was born in Aschersleben, Germany, on December 12, 1875. He came from a military family, and continued the tradition by joining the German Army on reaching adulthood. He fought in WWI, finishing up as a major with the position of divisional chief of staff. He remained in the army after the war ended, and rose through the ranks, becoming commander of the 3rd Infantry Division in 1932.

Rundstedt was involved in several events that involved political matters, including a threatened resignation when Franz von Papen declared martial law, and blocking the appointment of the pro-Nazi Walther von Reichenau as commander of the German Army. Rundstedt's unease with the rise of Nazism came to a head on October 31, 1938, when he resigned his post.

When war broke out, he was recalled to serve in the army, and in September 1939, took part in the invasion of Poland, leading the Army Group South. Having seen how quickly the German forces over-ran Poland, he supported Manstein's plan to invade

progress was slow compared with that of many other German army groups, but he played an important part in the capture of Kiev, helping take 665,000 Russian prisoners. He then moved his forces eastwards to attack Kharkov and Rostov. When the harsh Russian winter was looming, he tried to get Hitler to stop the advance until Spring, however, the Führer would not listen and the offensive continued.

In spite of suffering a heart attack in early November 1941, Rundstedt carried on leading his men towards Rostov. They reached the city on November 21, 1941, but were beaten back by the Red Army. Hitler was enraged by this and refused Rundstedt's demands to be allowed to withdraw. Instead the Führer sacked him, and replaced him with General Walther von Reichenau.

In March of the following year Hitler recalled him and tasked him with building fortifications along the coast of France, Belgium and Holland. These included the installation of large numbers of massive naval guns. After the Allies successfully staged the D-Day landings, Rundstedt tried to persuade Hitler to enter into peace negotiations, however, the Führer was not interested, and instead replaced him again, this time with General Gunther von Kluge.

France, and when the Western Offensive came he led seven Panzer divisions, three Motorized divisions, and 35 infantry divisions.

Although Rundstedt believed in the offensive, he was worried about the incredible pace of Guderian's tank units. He convinced Hitler to call a halt to proceedings until the infantry divisions had caught up with them. This misunderstanding of Blitzkrieg warfare allowed the British sufficient time to successfully evacuate their troops from Dunkirk. In spite of this, Rundstedt was promoted to field marshal on July 19, 1940, and helped with the planning of Operation "Sea Lion"—the invasion of Great Britain. When this was cancelled, he was tasked with commanding the occupation forces and coastal defences in France and the Low Countries.

When Operation "Barbarossa" was launched in June 1941, Rundstedt commanded the Army Group South; this was comprised of 52 infantry divisions and five panzer divisions. His

Although he had fallen foul of Hitler several times, he still agreed to stand on the board of the Army Court of Honor which purged the German Army after the July Plot to assassinate the Führer. He was captured by the Americans on May 1, 1945, and suffered another heart attack whilst being interrogated. He survived this and was eventually released in July 1948, after which he lived in Hanover until he died on February 24, 1953.

Walter Schellenberg

Born at Saarbrücken, Germany on January 16, 1910, Walter Schellenberg rose to become one of the Third Reich's top counter-intelligence specialists. He took medicine and law when he started his studies at the University of Bonn in 1929, and in May 1933 became a member of the Schutz Staffel (SS). His active mind impressed his superiors, and he was promoted many times whilst working in counter-intelligence operations. He also spent much of his time working to uncover plots against the regime and to identify those who were stirring up internal resistance. He worked alongside Reinhard Heydrich after Czechoslovakia was invaded, and was the leader of operations against the Soviet spy network, known as the Red Orchestra. When Heydrich was assassinated,

Schellenberg hoped to be appointed as his successor as head of the security services, but was bitterly disappointed when the position was given to Ernst Kaltenbrunner instead.

Towards the end of the war he went to Stockholm and tried to start negotiating a peace settlement with the Allies. This attempt failed, and he was arrested in June 1945. He testified against many other Nazis at the Nuremberg War Crimes Trial, and helped provide information to the British intelligence services about Soviet spying activities. He was sentenced to six years in prison in April 1949, during which time he wrote his memoirs. When it was discovered that he was seriously ill with a liver condition he was released after only two years. He died shortly after on March 31, 1952, in Turin, Italy.

Hugo Sperrle

Hugo Sperrle was born in Ludwigsburg, Germany, on February 7, 1885. Although his father was in the brewing industry, he joined the German Army in 1903 as an ensign in the infantry. He transferred to the German Army Air Service when WWI started, where he was an air observer throughout the war. He then joined the Freikorps, and when the Versailles Treaty prevented Germany from having an air force he rejoined the German Army.

He was promoted many times, and when Göring officially announced the creation of the Luftwaffe, Sperrle immediately left the army and joined it as a major general. When the Condor Legion was sent to Spain, he was placed in command of it. One of the first things he did was ensure that the latest aircraft would

be supplied to him when they came off the production lines. As a result the Condor Legion performed exceptionally well, and took part in all the major engagements of the Spanish Civil War.

He returned to Germany in October 1937, where he was appointed as commander of Air Fleet 3. In this role he made a major contribution to the blitzkrieg tactics used to such good effect in the Western Offensive. He was made air commander in the west in May 1941, and remained in France until after the D-Day landings in Normandy in June 1944. His failure to prevent the Allied invasion saw him dismissed from office. As a senior military figure he was charged with war crimes at the Nuremberg Trials, but was acquitted of all charges. Hugo Sperrle died in Munich on April 4, 1953.

Kurt Student

Kurt Student was born in Birkhonz, Germany, on May 12, 1890. He was commissioned in the German Army in 1912, and then moved over to the German Army Air Service. When WWI started, he flew reconnaissance and bombing missions, but when the Versailles Treaty banned the German air forces after the war ended, he rejoined the army. He left the army and in 1934 joined the fledgling Luftwaffe, helping build it into a significant air force.

Opening ceremony for the 1935 Nuremberg Rally. The front row (from left to right) is composed of: Himmler, Lutze, Hitler, Hess and Streicher.

He was promoted to major general in 1938, whereupon he was tasked with creating Germany's first parachute battalion. This airborne force was named the 7th Air Division, and although it could have been used in Poland, Hitler decided to keep the unit's existence secret until the start of the Western Offensive.

In 1940 Student's paratroopers were used to good effect in Norway, Belgium and the Netherlands. During the landings around the Hague and Rotterdam, where some 4,000 parachutists were dropped, Student was shot in the head; this kept him out of action until January 1941. It was intended that his paratroopers would play an important par t in Operation "Sea Lion"—the invasion of Great Britain, however, these plans were dropped when the operation was cancelled. It was also intended that his airborne troops would invade Gibraltar after Spain's General Franco refused to allow the German Army to cross his country.

When the invasion of Crete was launched between May 20 and June 1, 1941, the attack came from the air, however, 4,000 German paratroopers were killed in the assault. Many of these fatalities were the result of the troop-carrying gliders crashing before they ever reached their drop zones. Hitler was shocked by the numbers killed and decreed that large-scale airborne landings would no longer be used. This resulted in the cancellation of the invasion of Malta, and the conversion of the parachutists into ground troops. These elite soldiers were sent into action in Italy, Belgium, Holland and France during 1944, and then were used in a vain attempt to stop the Allies reaching the Rhine.

Adolf Hitler named Student to replace Gotthard Heinrici as commander of Army Group Vistula shortly before he shot himself. Kurt Student survived the war and eventually died in 1978.

Chronology of World War II

	1938
March 11	Anschluss — German annexation of Austria.
September 29	Munich Agreement signed.
October 5	Germany occupies Sudetenland.

	1939
March 14	Slovakia declares its independence.
March 31	Britain and France give guarantee to Poland.
April 7	Italy invades Albania.
May 22	Germany and Italy sign Pact of Steel.
August 23	Molotov-Ribbentrop pact signed between Germany and the Soviet Union.
September 1	Germany invades Poland.
September 1	Britain and France declare war on Germany.
September 17	Soviet Union invades Poland.
November 30	Soviet Union at war with Finland.

	1940
March 12	War between Soviet Union and Finland ends.
April 9	Germany invades Norway and Denmark.
April 14	Allied troops land in Norway.
May 10	Fall Gelb, the offensive in the West, is launched by Germany.
May 10	Churchill becomes Prime Minister of Great Britain.
May 14	Dutch Army surrenders.
May 26	Beginning of evacuation of Dunkirk.
May 28	Belgium surrenders.
June 2	Allies withdraw from Norway.
June 4	Dunkirk evacuation complete.
June 10	Italy declares war on Britain and France.
June 14	Germans enter Paris.
June 21	Italy launches offensive against France.
June 22	France and Germany sign armistice.
June 24	France and Italy sign armistice.
July 3	Royal Navy attacks French fleet at Mers el Kebir.
July 10	Beginning of the Battle of Britain.
September 17	Operation Sealion (the invasion of England) postponed by Hitler.
September 21	Italy and Germany sign Tripartite Pact.
September 27	Japan signs Tripartite Pact.
November 20	Hungary signs Tripartite Pact.
November 22	Romania signs Tripartite Pact.
November 23	Slovakia signs Tripartite Pact.

	1941
January 19	British launch East African campaign offensive.
January 22	Australian troops take Tobruk.
February 6	British capture Benghazi.
February 11	Rommel arrives in Libya.

March 25	Yugoslavia signs Tripartite Pact.
March 27	Yugoslavia leaves Tripartite Pact after coup d'etat.
March 28	Successful British naval action against Italians off Cape Matapan.
April 6–8	Axis forces invade Yugoslavia and Greece.
April 11	U.S.A. extends its naval neutrality patrols.
April 13	Belgrade falls to Axis forces.
April 14	Yugoslav forces surrender.
April 22	Greek First Army surrenders at Metsovan Pass.
May 16	Italians surrender to British at Amba Alagi.
May 20	Germans land on Crete.
May 24	H.M.S. Hood sunk by Bismarck.
May 27	Bismarck sunk by Royal Navy.
June 1	British withdraw from Crete.
June 2	Germany launches Operation Barbarossa against the Soviet Union.
July 27	Japanese troops invade French Indo-China.
September 19	Germans capture Kiev.
September 28	Three-power Conference in Moscow.
December 6	Britain declares war on Finland, Hungary and Rumania.
December 7	Japanese attack Pearl Harbor.
December 8	U.S.A. and Britain declare war on Japan.
December 8	Japanese invade Malaya and Thailand.
December 11	Germany and Italy declare war on the U.S.A.
December 14	Japanese begin invasion of Burma.
December 25	Japanese take Hong Kong.
1942	
February 15	Japanese troops capture Singapore from British.
February 27	Battle of the Java Sea.
February 28	Japanese invade Java.
March 8	Japanese invade New Guinea.
March 17	General MacArthur appointed to command South-West Pacific.
April 9	U.S. troops surrender in Bataan.
April 16	George Cross awarded to Island of Malta by H.R.H. King George VI.
April 26	Anglo-Soviet Treaty signed.
May 6	Japanese take Corregidor.
May 7	Battle of the Coral Sea.
May 20	British troops withdraw from Burma.
May 26	Rommel's Afrika Korps attack British at Gazala.
May 30	Royal Air Force launches first thousand-bomber raid on Germany.
June 4	Battle of Midway.
June 21	Rommel's Afrika Korps take Tobruk.
July 1	Sevastopol taken by Germans.
July 1	First Battle of El Alamein.
August 7	U.S. troops land on Guadalcanal.
August 11	PEDESTAL convoy arrives in Malta.
August 19	Raid on Dieppe.

August 31	Battle of Alam Halfa.
October 24	Second Battle of El Alamein.
November 8	Operation TORCH landings in North Africa.
November 11	Germans and Italians occupy Vichy France.
November 27	French fleet scuttled at Toulon.
1943	
January 14–24	Allied Conference at Casablanca.
January 23	British troops take Tripoli.
February 2	Germans surrender at Stalingrad.
February 8	Red Army captures Kursk.
February 13	Chindits launch first operation into Burma.
February 19	Battle for the Kasserine Pass.
April 19	First Warsaw rising.
April 19	Bermuda Conference.
May 11–25	TRIDENT conference in Washington.
May 13	Axis forces surrender in North Africa.
May 16	Royal Air Force "Dambuster" raid on Mohne and Eder dams.
May 24	U-boats withdraw from North Atlantic.
July 5	Battle of Kursk.
July 10	Allies land in Sicily.
July 25	Mussolini resigns.
September 3	Allies land on Italian mainland.
September 8	Surrender of Italy announced.
September 9	Allies land at Salerno.
September 10	Germans occupy Rome and Northern Italy.
October 13	Italy declares war on Germany.
November 6	Red Army captures Kiev.
November	First Allied conference in Cairo. 23–26
November 28–December 1	Allied conference in Teheran.
December 3–7	Second Allied conference in Cairo.
December 24	General Eisenhower promoted to supreme commander for OVERLORD, the Normandy landings.
1944	
January 22	Allies land at Anzio.
January 27	Red Army raises Siege of Leningrad.
January 31	U.S. forces land on Marshall Islands.
February 1	Battle for Monte Cassino begins.
March 2	Second Chindit operation into Burma.
May 11	Fourth Battle of Monte Cassino.
June 4	U.S. troops enter Rome.
June 6	Operation OVERLORD — Allied landings in Normandy.
June 19	Battle of the Philippine Sea.
July 1	Breton Woods conference.
July 20	Failed attempt to assassinate Hitler — July Bomb plot.
August 1	Second Warsaw rising.
August 4	Allied troops enter Florence.

August 15	Operation DRAGOON — Allied landings in southern France.
August 25	Germans in Paris surrender.
September 4	British troops capture Antwerp.
September	OCTAGON — Allied conference at Quebec. 12–16
September 17	Operation MARKET GARDEN at Arnhem.
September 21	Dumbarton Oaks conference.
October 14	British enter Athens.
October 23	De Gaulle recognised by Britain and U.S.A. as head of French Provisional Government.
October 24	Battle of Leyte Gulf.
December 16	Germans launch campaign in the Ardennes.
1945	
January 4–13	Japanese Kamikaze planes sink 17 U.S. ships and damage 50 more.
January 14	Red Army advances into East Prussia.
January 17	Red Army takes Warsaw.
January 30–February 3	First ARGONAUT Allied conference at Malta.
February 4–11	Second ARGONAUT Allied conference at Malta.
February 6	Allies clear Colmar pocket.
February 19	U.S. forces land on Iwo Jima.
February 26	U.S. 9th Army reaches Rhine.
March 7	U.S. 3rd Army crosses Rhine at Remagen Bridge.
March 20	British capture Mandalay.
March 30	Red Army enters Austria.
April 1	U.S. First and Ninth Armies encircle the Ruhr.
April 1	U.S. forces land on Okinawa.
April 12	President Roosevelt dies and Truman becomes president.
April 13	Red Army takes Vienna.
April 25	U.S. and Soviet forces meet at Torgau.
April 28	Mussolini shot by partisans.
April 29	Germans sign surrender terms for troops in Italy.
April 30	Hitler commits suicide.
May 2	Red Army takes Berlin.
May 3	British enter Rangoon.
May 4	German forces in the Netherlands, northern Germany and Denmark surrender to General Montgomery on Luneburg Heath.
May 5	Germans in Norway surrender.
May 7	General Alfred Jodl signs unconditional surrender of Germany at Reims, to take effect on May 9.
May 8	Victory in Europe Day.
May 10	Red Army takes Prague.
July 17–August 2	Allied TERMINAL conference held in Potsdam.
July 26	Winston Churchill resigns after being defeated in the general election. Clement Attlee becomes Prime Minister of Great Britain.
August 6	Atomic bomb dropped on Hiroshima.
August 8	Soviet Union declares war on Japan.
August 9	Atomic bomb dropped on Nagasaki.
August 14	Unconditional surrender of Japanese forces announced by Emperor Hirohito.
August 15	Victory in Japan Day.
September 2	Japanese sign surrender aboard U.S.S. Missouri in Tokyo Bay.